The Academic Book of the Future

Other Palgrave Pivot titles

Ben Clements: Surveying Christian Beliefs and Religious Debates in Post-War Britain

Robert A. Stebbins: Leisure and the Motive to Volunteer: Theories of Serious, Casual, and Project-Based Leisure

Dietrich Orlow: Socialist Reformers and the Collapse of the German Democratic Republic

Gwendolyn Audrey Foster: Disruptive Feminisms: Raced, Gendered, and Classed Bodies in Film

Catherine A. Lugg: US Public Schools and the Politics of Queer Erasure

Olli Pyyhtinen: More-than-Human Sociology: A New Sociological Imagination

Jane Hemsley-Brown and Izhar Oplatka: Higher Education Consumer Choice

Arthur Asa Berger: Gizmos or: The Electronic Imperative: How Digital Devices have Transformed American Character and Culture

Antoine Vauchez: Democratizing Europe

Cassie Smith-Christmas: Family Language Policy: Maintaining an Endangered Language in the Home

Liam Magee: Interwoven Cities

Alan Bainbridge: On Becoming an Education Professional: A Psychosocial Exploration of Developing an Education Professional Practice

Bruce Moghtader: Foucault and Educational Ethics

Carol Rittner and John K. Roth: Teaching about Rape in War and Genocide

Robert H. Blank: Cognitive Enhancement: Social and Public Policy Issues

Cathy Hannabach: Blood Cultures: Medicine, Media, and Militarisms

Adam Bennett, G. Russell Kincaid, Peter Sanfey, and Max Watson: Economic and Policy Foundations for Growth in South East Europe: Remaking the Balkan Economy

Shaun May: Rethinking Practice as Research and the Cognitive Turn

Eoin Price: 'Public' and 'Private' Playhouses in Renaissance England: The Politics of Publication

David Elliott: Green Energy Futures: A Big Change for the Good

palgrave▶pivot

The Academic Book of the Future

Edited by

Rebecca E. Lyons
Research Associate, University College London, UK

and

Samantha J. Rayner
Senior Lecturer in Publishing, University College London, UK

 Except where otherwise noted, this work is licensed under a Creative Commons Attribution 4.0 International License. To view a copy of this license, visit https://creativecommons.org/version4

DOI: 10.1057/9781137595775.0001

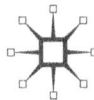

THE ACADEMIC BOOK OF THE FUTURE
Selection, Introduction and editorial matter copyright © Rebecca E. Lyons and Samantha J. Rayner, 2016.
Individual chapters copyright © the contributors, 2016.
All rights reserved.
Open access:

 This work is licensed under a Creative Commons Attribution 4.0 International License. The images or other third party material in this article are included in the work's Creative Commons license, unless indicated otherwise in the credit line; if the material is not included under the Creative Commons license, users will need to obtain permission from the license holder to reproduce the material. To view a copy of this license, visit http://creativecommons.org/licenses/by/4.0/

First published 2016 by
PALGRAVE MACMILLAN

The authors have asserted their rights to be identified as the authors of this work in accordance with the Copyright, Designs and Patents Act 1988.

Palgrave Macmillan in the UK is an imprint of Macmillan Publishers Limited, registered in England, company number 785998, of Houndmills, Basingstoke, Hampshire, RG21 6XS.

Palgrave Macmillan in the US is a division of Nature America, Inc., One New York Plaza, Suite 4500 New York, NY 10004–1562.

Palgrave Macmillan is the global academic imprint of the above companies and has companies and representatives throughout the world.

Hardback ISBN: 978–1–137–59576–8
E-PUB ISBN: 978–1–137–59578–2
E-PDF ISBN: 978–1–137–59577–5
DOI: 10.1057/9781137595775

Distribution in the UK, Europe and the rest of the world is by Palgrave Macmillan®, a division of Macmillan Publishers Limited, registered in England, company number 785998, of Houndmills, Basingstoke, Hampshire RG21 6XS.

Names: Lyons, Rebecca E., 1986- editor. | Rayner, Samantha J., editor.

Title: The academic book of the future / [selected and edited by] Rebecca E. Lyons, Research Associate, University College London, UK ; Samantha J. Rayner, Senior Lecturer in Publishing, University College London, UK.

Description: New York: Palgrave Macmillan, 2015. | Includes bibliographical references and index.

Identifiers: LCCN 2015037749 | ISBN 9781137595768 (hardback)

Subjects: LCSH: Scholarly publishing. | Academic writing. | Open access publishing. | Textbooks—Authorship.

Classification: LCC Z286.S37 A35 2015 | DDC 070.5/94—dc23 LC record available at http://lccn.loc.gov/2015037749

A catalogue record for this book is available from the British Library.

A catalog record for this book is available from the Library of Congress.

Contents

Acknowledgements   vii

Notes on Contributors   ix

Introduction: The Academic Book of the Future   1
Rebecca E. Lyons and Samantha J. Rayner

Part I   Academics

1   The Academic Book as Socially-Embedded Media Artefact   11
Tom Mole

2   Wearable Books   18
Michael Pidd

3   The Impossible Constellation: Practice as Research as a Viable Alternative   24
Sarah Barrow

Part II   Publishers

4   The Academic Book of the Future and the Need to Break Boundaries   32
Jenny McCall and Amy Bourke-Waite

5   The Academic 'Book' of the Future and Its Function   39
Frances Pinter

6	The University Press and the Academic Book of the Future *Anthony Cond*	46

Part III Librarians

7	National Libraries and Academic Books of the Future *Maja Maricevic*	57
8	Strategic Engagement and Librarians *Neil Smyth*	66
9	Academic Libraries and Academic Books: Vessels of Cultural Continuity, Agents of Cultural Change *Kate Price*	74

Part IV Booksellers

10	Selling Words: An Economic History of Bookselling *Jaki Hawker*	84
11	The Future of the Academic Book: The Role of Booksellers *Peter Lake*	92
12	Back to the Future: The Role of the Campus Bookshop *Craig Dadds*	98

Bibliography	104
Further Reading	114
Index	118

Acknowledgements

This book would not exist without the incredible hard work, dedication and enthusiasm of all 13 contributors. First and foremost, credit must be given to them. They worked to some fairly improbable deadlines, yet each delivered everything punctually and – equally as importantly – with grace, good humour, and a sympathetic understanding of the book and its aims, as well as the wider Project. Their chapters are honest, thought-provoking, and important – resounding with experience and expertise. For this, and for so much else, we thank them.

Palgrave Macmillan must be thanked next. This Palgrave Pivot was their idea, and a risk, but the whole team there has been completely supportive throughout the entire process. Their willingness to experiment, and dedication to participating in the conversation has enabled this book to happen, and has made for a professional end result – just as an academic book should be. No stage in the rigorous reviewing process has been skipped, and people have committed to working round the clock to get the book ready for Academic Book Week. We would especially like to thank Jen McCall, who has been a marvel! Also Lauren Pettifer for the marketing, April James and Tomas René for the editorial support, and Philippa Grand, Caitlin Cornish and Katharine Nelson for the first conversation with the Project team where the initial idea for 'a book in a week' was suggested!

We'd also like to acknowledge the support we had for printing the first copies of the book, and for taking on distribution: to David Taylor, Andrew Bromley and all at

Ingram Lightning Source – we are hugely grateful for your vital input into this project!

Finally, I would like to thank the person who does, perhaps, more than any of the rest of us involved in this volume, represent the academic book of the future: our Research Associate, Rebecca Lyons. She has project-managed the stages of the book to submission of the manuscript, communicated with speed and efficiency (and unflagging good temper) to all involved, edited with tact and skill, and shown exceptional multi-tasking talents in juggling this with all the other Project activity. With a background in publishing, but now in the final stages of writing her own PhD, Rebecca shows what the academic of the future will be like, and it is very impressive: thank you, Bex, for everything!

We have been incredibly lucky to work with people who have given so generously of their time and shared their experienced perspectives: despite the cynicism that surrounds many of the contexts the wider Project is investigating, we are finding a huge amount of work out there that is positive, collaborative and innovative. So we are incredibly proud and excited to be a part of the conversation around the academic book of the future, and to have played a part in the publication of this book.

Samantha Rayner
September 2015

Notes on Contributors

Sarah Barrow, Head, School of Film and Media, University of Lincoln: As a media and film scholar who has published in the more traditional 'book' format, Sarah has always enjoyed the opportunities afforded by working with and championing film-maker, performance and artist colleagues and students. The perspective in her chapter draws also on experiences of cinema production, film education and festival programming. Since 2011, she has been part of the team that brings Frequency Festival of Digital Cultures to Lincoln, and in 2014 she jointly co-ordinated the Practice as Research festival/symposium The Impossible Constellation at Lincoln.

Amy Bourke-Waite, Senior Communications Manager, Palgrave Macmillan: Amy works in the communications team for Palgrave Macmillan and Nature Publishing Group, both part of newly formed company Springer Nature, a major new force in scientific, scholarly, professional and educational publishing. Amy has been involved in Palgrave Macmillan's Open Access monograph programme from its inception in 2013, and is fascinated by how Open Access book models are evolving in a challenging market, and how academics' perceptions of Open Access are changing over time.

Anthony Cond, Managing Director, Liverpool University Press: Anthony is the Managing Director of Liverpool University Press, the IPG Frankfurt Book Fair Academic and Professional Publisher of the Year 2015, and the Bookseller Independent Academic, Educational and

Professional Publisher of the Year 2015. He is a Director of the Association of Learned and Professional Society Publishers and an Honorary Fellow in the School of the Arts at the University of Liverpool.

Craig Dadds, University Bookshop Manager, Canterbury Christ Church University: Craig has worked in academic bookselling at Canterbury Christ Church University since 1998, and prior to that from 1989 managed a branch of Albion Bookshop, a small chain of independent booksellers in South East England.

Jaki Hawker, Academic Manager, Blackwell's Edinburgh: Jaki's years of involvement in web-based digital text development, academic bookselling and managing textbook sales in the second largest academic bookshop in the UK have provided her with a broad perspective on text, publishing and bookselling. In a challenging retail environment, a successful academic bookshop has to be proactive and knowledgeable about their customers and their market, identifying trends and supporting learning.

Peter Lake, Group Business Development Director, JS Group: Peter has worked in publishing and bookselling for the past 30 years. As a publisher, he worked for Pearson, Reed Elsevier and Thomson Reuters where he was CEO of the leading legal publisher Sweet & Maxwell. During his time at Sweet & Maxwell, the business transitioned from being a print publisher to an online database and services provider. As well as running publishing businesses in the UK, he has also run businesses in Asia, Europe and the Middle East. For the past four years he has worked at the JS Group. The JS Group has two principal areas of activity: on campus, bookselling under the John Smith's brand and providing solutions for governments and universities to distribute financial and other support to students with the Aspire range of services. JS Group is also working very closely on the development and deployment of the Kortext eBook platform.

Maja Maricevic, Head of Higher Education, The British Library: Maja is responsible for the British Library's strategic relationships and developments with the higher education sector. In this role she is responsible for the Library's collaboration with the Alan Turing Institute, the UK's new national institute for data sciences, which has its headquarters at The British Library. She is leading on the development of The British Library's relations with FutureLearn, the UK's largest MOOC provider, and has worked over a number of years to broaden the Library's postgraduate programme. She leads The British Library's collaborative work with the AHRC that has led to The Academic Book of the Future Project. She is actively involved with the Project as a member of the Advisory and Strategy Boards. She is also a member of the Universities UK Open Access Implementation Group, and a member of the RCUK Advisory Group, which is currently working to develop the RCUK Concordat on Open Research Data.

Jenny McCall, Global Head of Humanities, Palgrave Macmillan: Jen manages Palgrave Macmillan's humanities editorial team, and has overall responsibility for Palgrave's publishing portfolio of monographs, edited collections, handbooks and Palgrave Pivots covering literature, history, philosophy, theatre and performance studies, culture and media studies, and film studies. Latterly she has been working to develop Palgrave's Campaign for the Humanities: http://www.palgrave.com/page/humanities-campaign/

Tom Mole, Reader in English Literature and Director of the Centre for the History of the Book, University of Edinburgh: Tom is the author or editor of four academic books, including *Byron's Romantic Celebrity* (2007) and the *Broadview Reader in Book History* (2014). The Centre for the History of the Book, which he leads, was founded in 1995 to support advanced research into all aspects of the production, circulation and reception of books. In particular, he focuses on how understanding the history of the book in relation to past moments of media change can inform current debates about the future of the book.

Michael Pidd, Digital Director, HRI Digital, University of Sheffield: Michael has more than 20 years of experience in developing, managing and delivering collaborative research projects in the digital humanities. He believes that we are in a period of transformation, as all traditional aspects of academic book production and consumption are being challenged. In his view, understanding what the future of the academic book might be like is critical to understanding what the future of academic discourse might be like.

Frances Pinter, CEO, Manchester University Press and Founder, Knowledge Unlatched: Frances has been a publisher of scholarly books for several decades – publishing thousands of monographs over the years. She worked for the Open Society Foundation and saw first-hand the thirst for access to scholarly books around the world. She is the founder of Knowledge Unlatched.

Kate Price, Associate Director (Collections & Research Support), King's College London: Kate is responsible for strategic leadership across a diverse range of activities, including the provision of support for the research community in moving towards Open Access publication and the effective management of research data; the timely and cost effective procurement and cataloguing of library materials in all formats; and the management of the nationally significant Special Collections and Archives housed at King's. She is currently Chair of UKSG, an organisation that exists to connect the knowledge community and encourage the exchange of ideas on scholarly communication. Along with Virginia Havergal, she co-edited *E-books in Libraries: A Practical Guide*, published by Facet in February 2011.

Neil Smyth, Senior Librarian, Faculty of Arts, University of Nottingham: Before taking up his current post, Neil was the Arts Faculty Team Leader. Based in the Hallward Library, he is responsible for working with senior representatives in the Arts Faculty to shape the strategic direction of library services. His perspectives on the academic book come from working in a university library, where he is surrounded by academic books and, perhaps more importantly, current and future authors of books.

OPEN

Introduction: The Academic Book of the Future

Rebecca E. Lyons and Samantha J. Rayner

Lyons, Rebecca E. and Samantha J. Rayner (eds). *The Academic Book of the Future*. Basingstoke: Palgrave Macmillan, 2016. DOI: 10.1057/9781137595775.0004.

In early 2014, the Arts and Humanities Research Council (AHRC) partnered with The British Library to launch a call for teams to run The Academic Book of the Future Project. The Project brief was 'to explore the future of the academic book in the context of Open Access publishing and the digital revolution'.[1] Our team[2] successfully pitched to facilitate a two-pronged approach. We are using the expert services of the Research Information Network and Dr Michael Jubb to undertake a wide-ranging series of focus groups, gathering responses to our research questions,[3] whilst the core Project team are consulting with the communities of practice connected to academic books to evoke responses via more detailed pieces of commissioned research, symposia, workshops and conferences. The mid-point of the Project, Academic Book Week (9–16 November, 2015),[4] will highlight a week-long showcase of this activity, plus other special events from our partners, including the launch of the volume you are now reading.

Books matter. They contain knowledge, and knowledge, as the saying goes, is power. Over the centuries, control of the production of texts has been (and in some places still is) manipulated by governments, by religious groups and by those who fought (and those who are still fighting) for their wider, more openly accessible distribution. Books *are* matter: they are containers, crucibles, confrontations. They can teach, guide, inspire, soothe, and agitate. They can exist physically or digitally. Trying to define what a book is, or could be, is a challenging task: it exists in so many different guises, and is always finding new ways to reinvent itself. Our Project seeks rather to try and curate a map of these many guises, underlining the strength in the diversity of choice available to the author, whilst highlighting the challenges of production, distribution, use and preservation that these choices bring.

Academic books, at least in the UK, have a currency as part of the Research Excellence Framework (REF), which measures the quality of academic research. There is, therefore, a pressure to understand the map of academic publishing in its entirety. Given that scholarly communication operates on a global stage, with different countries having different (or no) national assessment systems, and that books (physical or digital) circulate in ways that are difficult to track, the Project team acknowledges that as cartographers, the most impact they can have on that map is to log and analyse some key landscape features. Engaging with so many different agents in the academic book circuit has enabled us to appreciate their widespread willingness to collaborate and their curiosity to learn from what others have done or experienced. The small volume that you hold in your hands or are reading on a screen therefore represents a mighty amount of energy and commitment to the academic book – to all academic books, in their past, present and future states. The contributors have worked together with the teams at Palgrave and the AHRC/British Library Academic Book of the Future Project to produce a witness to the extraordinary – and relevant – set of talents and experiences, ideas and reflections that connect people who inhabit the communities of practice that form the contexts of the academic book.

This publication

An initial conversation with Palgrave Macmillan in March 2015 resulted in the challenge to create a Palgrave Pivot for Academic Book Week. The original suggestion – to create a book in a week – was modified to an attempt to go from commissioning to production to distribution in a rapid time frame: a Palgrave Pivot.[5] Contributors were shortlisted from across the Project's four main stakeholder areas: publishing, libraries, academia and bookselling. A proposal was submitted by the Project team to Palgrave, and was sent off for review. The authors were approached and chapters commissioned in late July 2015. The proposal reviews came back just before first chapter drafts were due to be submitted, and in late August 2015 all of the authors submitted their chapters. Review and editing were undertaken by Rebecca Lyons, Samantha Rayner and Palgrave's Jen McCall, and with a turnaround of roughly one week, the chapters were back with their authors for amendments. The existence of this book owes a great deal to the unfailing dedication of each of the 13 contributors, who worked to extremely tight deadlines to expedite the crucial commissioning, editing and review stages.

It is fitting that this volume begins with the perspective of a book historian: no foray into the future should ignore the contexts of the past. Dr Tom Mole, Reader in English Literature and Director of the Centre for the History of the Book at the University of Edinburgh, suggests that whatever shapes or formats books might take in the future, their most important role will continue to be their 'transformative contributions to knowledge' (p. 16). Whilst digital technology affords new possibilities in terms of research and dissemination, it might also have drawbacks in terms of readers' engagement with, and comprehension of, the text. Mole reminds us of the usefulness of the printed codex, and the 'need to ensure that the most valuable qualities of the academic book as printed codex migrate to the new media environment without being devalued' (p. 16).

The next chapter moves from the past into an imagined future. In his satirical dystopia, Michael Pidd, Digital Director for HRI Digital at the University of Sheffield, describes a future in which books are wearable: smart lenses that project data onto the back of our eyelids, networked chips embedded into our hands to 'summon sheets of interactive v-paper', and Data Projection Gloves (p. 19). In this iteration of the future, the academic book has reached optimum levels of media-embedded, holistic, user-friendly interactivity. But the biggest innovation of all is the concept of 'Linked Ideas'. Books, articles and other research outputs have lost all their old distinction, because ideas on a topic can automatically be 'located, retrieved and assembled' from amongst 'all written discourse' (p. 10). 'Like' and 'dislike' indicators and a 'comment' facility are used for the peer-review process, and the need to submit books for assessment is obsolete. But does this vision of the future satisfy?

Dr Sarah Barrow, Head of the School of Film and Media at the University of Lincoln, moves the academic section towards an examination of the challenging issues of Practice as Research, and considers the academic book of the future in terms of research that does not conform to purely textual outputs. Barrow argues against the prioritisation or fetishisation of text over other forms of research output, and seeks to eliminate the walls between theory and practice, pointing to the video essay as a potential format that enables such work. There is a need, she argues, to 'trust in alternative ways of doing and presenting research' – the academic book of the future should be allowed to be 'other' (p. 25). But, she goes on to highlight, changes in policy and evaluation exercises will be required to enable and facilitate such otherness.

The needs of academics have shifted, but publishing and its processes and products have also changed. Developments such as print on demand – as well as huge shifts in digital affordances – have offered publishers new freedoms, such as in the format and platforms for ebooks and other digital content, and the ability to publish titles in smaller print runs for lower costs. This has coincided with changes in the way that academics research and write their books. In their chapter, Jenny McCall, Global

Head of Humanities, and Amy Bourke-Waite, Senior Communications Manager, at Palgrave Macmillan discuss the Palgrave Pivot format, and the motivation behind its development within these contexts.

The function of the academic book will be just as important as its form, argues Dr Frances Pinter, CEO of Manchester University Press and Founder of Knowledge Unlatched. The 'scaffolding' (p. 40) around academic books, including business models, supply chains, metadata and digital tools, will require special attention. In the evolution of the academic book, it will be 'knowledge infrastructures' (p. 40) that are key: the 'ecology of people, practices, technologies, institutions, material objects and their relationships within each discipline'.[6] Interdisciplinarity will increase as digital affordances not only provide answers to old questions, but also encourage new questions to be asked. Delivery and discovery systems for ebooks will have to improve. And publishers, she says, will have to move with the times.

Anthony Cond, the Managing Director of Liverpool University Press, highlights the inextricable links between the university press (UP) and academia. A UP reports to its university library, senior university managers or quasi-university committees: it is 'a mirror to the budgetary, utility and reputational concerns of the subjects and institution it serves' (p. 47). But Cond is fairly confident about the place of UPs in new and emerging landscapes and contexts. Open Access and digital materials seem an inevitable part of the academic book of the future, but Cond holds that the 'esteem of the university press brand and the rigour of university press peer review' (p. 50) will be crucial – perhaps more so than ever. The academic book may have several possible futures, but, Cond says, the need for 'credentialisation' (p. 43) will remain a constant.

The close relationship between national libraries, researchers and academic books has not altered in its essence despite huge contextual changes, such as digital developments, says Maja Maricevic, Head of Higher Education at The British Library. However, researchers' 'reading and information seeking behaviours' (p. 59) have shifted, with Google becoming the most-used research channel. In such contexts, national libraries will be pivotal for their preservation role, with researcher access being provided through other channels. National libraries will also become increasingly useful for their role in preserving digital collections outside of scholarly publishing: non-academic ebooks, online newspapers, growing audio and video collections, web archives and digitised heritage collections. Going forward, Maricevic suggests, a stronger relationship between funders, policy-makers and other national libraries will be a key aspect of The British Library's role, as well as a willingness to experiment with new ways of working – this Project being a key example of this kind of initiative.

Neil Smyth, Senior Librarian of the Faculty of Arts at the University of Nottingham, also considers the possible strategic issues and opportunities surrounding the academic book of the future – with regard to university libraries. The expansion in book format options from physical to digital; the changing roles of academics and librarians, and the consequently shifting relationships between the two groups; and the importance of academic books to the REF and university funding all have massive implications for the role of university libraries. How, asks Smyth, will academic books be organised and accessed in the future, if they are not in libraries? What conversations should take place between academics and librarians around academic books? What is the place of libraries in processes such as the REF? And finally, how can libraries best support the academic authors of the future: the students?

Kate Price, Associate Director (Collections & Research Support) at King's College London, broadens the focus to consider the academic book beyond the academy. As agents of cultural change, the reach of academic books is wide, transforming knowledge and perceptions (consider Darwin, for example), and influencing cultural attitudes as their content and ideas disseminate. Price considers the social and technological barriers to accessing academic books; the potential volatility of digital content (issues with archiving social media, for instance), and the role that libraries might play in these issues in the future. Price calls libraries agents of cultural continuity, providing access to current and past thought, as well as the threads of reasoning linking the two, and examines the implications in an Open Access future where the academic book is entirely 'de-coupled from the concept of the library collection' (p. 78).

Jaki Hawker, Academic Manager of Blackwell's Edinburgh, views the future of the academic book in terms of demand and supply. 'For me,' Hawker states, 'the bottom line in considering the academic book of the future is not "What does it look like?" but "Does it sell?"' (p. 89). The consumer will shape the academic book of the future, which will be 'inclusive, collaborative, available across multiple platforms and in a number of formats' (p. 90). Given innovations such as Open Access, print on demand and learning platform development, it seems that the academic book of the future has infinite possibilities. And maybe it does. But Hawker argues that they will be 'created, enabled and shaped by the market' (p. 90).

Peter Lake, Group Business Development Director of the John Smith Group, focuses on a particular type of academic book: the undergraduate textbook. Traditionally the staple for academic publishers, this type of academic book is in decline in the face of major sea-changes in the ways that universities deliver their courses, and the ways in which publishers are catering for them. Universities often now create their own materials – materials that increasingly replace textbooks – including Massive Open Online Courses (MOOCs), online lectures and other digital resources. Publishers are creating new solutions too, blending 'traditional textbook content with adaptive learning technologies, embedded testing and assessment features, integrated assignment functionality, personal study wallets and records, and collaborative learning tools' (p. 94). 'So,' Lake asks, 'if the university bookseller is going to be selling fewer textbooks, what will its role be in the future?' (p. 94). The bookseller of the future may very well assist in the discovery of resources 'from multiple providers and in multiple formats' (p. 95); create and maintain digital content platforms; and take an active part in analytics and evaluation services.

Craig Dadds, the University Bookshop Manager at Canterbury Christ Church University, considers the campus bookshop and its relationship with the people and contexts in which academic books are written and used. For Dadds, the campus bookshop is key to the cultural life of the university, the student and staff experience, and the options and opportunities available to those within the university system. He is supported by a survey, undertaken at Canterbury Christ Church University (CCCU), of one hundred academics. When asked 'What are the benefits of an academic bookshop on campus?', responses cited the importance of the academic bookshop as a bridge between academia and the wider public, with open talks, book signings and other events playing a key role. CCCU's academics named the bookshop as a pivotal location for locating niche and specialist information with the support of knowledgeable staff. The bookshop is also an important symbol of 'academic rigour and learning' (p. 100) to those embedded within its contexts, as well as those without. In this chapter the bookshop emerges as a key player in the world of academic books, aiding not just in their dissemination, but assisting in their creation and reach into the wider world beyond academia.

DOI: 10.1057/9781137595775.0004

A launch pad for further conversations

The practice-based research process of creating this Palgrave Pivot has not only resulted in an output with an integrity that the uncompromised review procedures protected, but it has innovated in several different ways: the spread of authors across very different areas; the speed with which they composed and submitted their chapters; the work flows; and even the cover – which was chosen by a public vote. But the greatest innovation of this publication – what really makes it unique – is the conversations that have been and will be created around it. Read them individually, and the chapters in this volume are interesting, thought-provoking, insightful. Put them together, and suddenly new angles emerge: contexts shift, horizons broaden.

This volume serves as a launch pad for future conversations to take place. These will help to generate responses that will feed into and shape the second half of the Project's life, and they will also help to shape the wider conversations taking place around the academic book in broader areas, such as policy and government.

Professor Geoffrey Crossick ended his report *Monographs and Open Access* by remarking how impressed he had been by the willingness of the arts, humanities, and social science communities to engage with him, and urging: 'It is important that this engagement continues, because there is much to be gained by working with the grain, and much to be lost by not doing so.'[7] This Palgrave Pivot provides tangible proof (in hard copy and Open Access formats, and in the paratexts that have been created and collected around its production) that engagement is continuing via the AHRC/British Library Academic Book of the Future Project, and beyond. The future of the academic book is collaboration. The future of the academic book is in your hands.

Notes

1. See http://www.ahrc.ac.uk/funding/opportunities/current/academicbookofthefuture/ (accessed 6 September 2015).
2. The Project team consists of Dr Samantha Rayner (Principal Investigator, Centre for Publishing, UCL), Nick Canty (Co-Investigator, Centre for Publishing, UCL), Professor Marilyn Deegan (Co-Investigator, Department of Digital Humanities, King's College, London), Simon Tanner (Co-Investigator,

Department of Digital Humanities, King's College, London) and Rebecca Lyons (Research Associate, UCL).
3 See http://academicbookfuture.org/about-the-project/ (accessed 6 September 2015).
4 See http://acbookweek.com/ (accessed 6 September 2015).
5 See Jenny McCall and Amy Bourke-Waite, 'The Academic Book of the Future and the Need to Break Boundaries', Chapter 4 in this volume.
6 Christine Borgman (2015) *Big Data, Little Data, No Data* (Boston: MIT Press), p. 33.
7 G. Crossick (2014) *Monographs and Open Access*: A Report to HEFCE, http://www.hefce.ac.uk/media/hefce/content/pubs/indirreports/2015/Monographs,and,open,access/2014_monographs.pdf, accessed 20 August 2015, p. 70.

Except where otherwise noted, this work is licensed under a Creative Commons Attribution 4.0 International License. To view a copy of this license, visit https://creativecommons.org/version4

Part I
Academics

OPEN

1

The Academic Book as Socially-Embedded Media Artefact

Tom Mole

▶ **Abstract:** *For as long as it has existed in its modern form, the academic book has operated in what Jerome McGann calls 'a double helix of perceptual codes: the linguistic codes [...] and the bibliographical codes'. It unites a particular discursive genre with a particular material format. But now the double helix is starting to unravel as new, genetically modified digital formats force us to rethink what the academic book can be. This moment of media change meshes with shifts in the funding and assessment of research, developments in researchers' intellectual agendas and the challenges of Open Access. As disciplinary boundaries become more porous and scholarly outputs more varied, these changes will affect every stage in the life-cycle of the academic book.*

Keywords: academic book of the future; academic codex; assessment; book history; format; funding monograph; hiring; PhD thesis; promotion; research output; socially-embedded media artifact; the academy

Lyons, Rebecca E. and Samantha J. Rayner (eds).
The Academic Book of the Future. Basingstoke: Palgrave Macmillan, 2016. DOI: 10.1057/9781137595775.0006.

For as long as it has existed in its modern form as a printed codex, the academic book has operated in what Jerome McGann calls 'a double helix of perceptual codes: the linguistic codes [...] and the bibliographical codes'.[1] It unites a particular discursive genre with a particular material format. But now the double helix is starting to unravel as new, genetically modified digital formats force us to rethink what the academic book can be. This moment of media change meshes with shifts in the funding and assessment of research, developments in researchers' intellectual agendas and the challenges of Open Access. As disciplinary boundaries become more porous and scholarly outputs more varied, these changes will affect every stage in the life-cycle of the academic book, from research, collaboration and writing through publication, marketing, reading and preservation, whether it is a monograph, a scholarly edition, a collection of essays or a record of creative endeavour. Addressing the challenges the academic book of the future poses requires academics, librarians, publishers, funding councils, creative technologists, and research consumers to collaborate.

Intellectual work is starting to take on a variety of new forms, both as a result of scholars rethinking the best format in which to share their ideas, and as a result of external demands for transparent, measurable outputs. These shifts mandate a moment of self-reflection about the academic book. We can't afford to draw battle lines between the boosters of new technologies and the naysayers who cling to things as they were. Instead, we need a debate that is both historically informed and technologically literate. It should examine what new kinds of intellectual work the academic book of the future will make possible. But it should also consider what current features of the academic book are essential to excellent research and scholarship and should be preserved in the future. As we consider how field-changing work of lasting and transformative value in the humanities will be written, funded, rewarded, disseminated and preserved in a new media environment, we need to understand the affordances and limitations of the printed codex as an artefact of intellectual life. As the field that studies the production, circulation and reception of books as material artefacts in historical perspective, book history brings a distinctive approach to such debates. This short essay reflects this perspective by situating the academic book materially, institutionally and historically in order to understand what's at stake in its current transformation.

The current form of the academic book as a printed codex constrains arts and humanities researchers in various specific ways: scholars of screen media cannot include clips from films, TV programmes or computer games; cultural geographers cannot include dynamic interactive maps; art historians and scholars of visual culture cannot typically include large numbers of colour images; musicologists cannot include audio; researchers working with large data-sets cannot typically publish the data on which their arguments depend; textual editors cannot include all the documentary evidence they have assembled; scholars engaged in creative and performing arts research cannot always document their practice adequately. The processes of assessment and production are slow and post-publication revision is difficult. It should be possible to overcome some of these constraints when the academic book no longer (only) takes the form of a printed codex. This means that the academic book of the future must do more than remediate the printed codex, replicating the experience of paper books in digital formats as current e-readers typically do.

Even as the constraints of the printed codex become harder to ignore, systemic factors combine to pressure scholars to write more of them. Many North American universities that would not have required a monograph for tenure in humanities disciplines a decade ago now routinely look for one, while some that have always expected a monograph for tenure now expect to see significant progress towards a second book. In the UK, Research Excellence Framework (REF) panels tend to value monographs highly (and arguably to undervalue edited collections and scholarly editions). Monographs feature prominently in hiring and promotion decisions, increasing the pressure on scholars at all career stages to think of their work in terms of monograph publication.[2] At the same time, many academic presses are publishing fewer monographs – especially in certain disciplines such as modern languages – and are printing fewer copies of the monographs they do publish. Libraries buy fewer monographs, largely because they spend increasing fractions of their shrinking acquisitions budgets on bundled scientific journals published for profit. In these conditions we have to ask what the academic book is for.

Despite its limitations, the monograph has become a gold standard in many humanities disciplines for good reasons. The academic book's rise to the centre of our intellectual lives has its own long history. The codex and the architecture of the page have been built into the fabric of the academy and the careers of those who work there ever since the university system developed in the twelfth century.[3] The advent of printing helped produce the Renaissance's flowering of humanistic scholarship and the transformation of the academy it entailed.[4] With the massive proliferation of printed books at the end of the eighteenth century the modern research university took shape, as Chad Wellmon has argued, as an institution to control the production, dissemination, organisation and storage of books.[5] As the modern disciplinary organisation of knowledge emerged in the nineteenth century and then the higher education sector expanded in Europe and North America in the twentieth, the monograph became the most valued form of research output and, eventually, the signal achievement allowing access to senior positions in the profession. In these contexts, the monograph aimed to be the definitive statement of an author's work on a well-defined topic, reflecting a relatively ambitious research programme, typically carried out over several years, informed by a comprehensive grasp of existing work in the field, which reflected sustained intellectual effort at the highest level and aspired to produce a lasting contribution to knowledge.

Understanding the history of the academic monograph shows us that the printed academic codex is a socially-embedded media artefact, whose significance lies as much in the institutional and professional structures it helps to produce as in the technology of print itself.[6] The academic book has fostered assessment practices that assure quality, such as peer review, and add value, such as publishers' editing, design, layout, indexing and so on. These structures ensure that the prestige of the academic book is justified and they must be replicated or revised in the digital environment. The academic book has given rise to professional protocols that inform credentialing, hiring, promotion and reward decisions. While a PhD thesis differs in important ways from a published book, the shape of the doctorate mirrors the form of the monograph: a doctorate is in large part a course of training in how to write a book. The monograph has been connected to a marketing and dissemination apparatus that allows it to reach its audience effectively. It benefits from institutional structures and communities of practice, such as libraries within and beyond universities, that ensure its long-term preservation and accessibility. The academic book is and will remain embedded in social, professional and institutional structures that make it an effective research output. Changing the form of the academic book will mean changing those structures in order for them to remain fit for purpose. If our current moment of media change is to enrich and empower humanistic scholarship rather than cheapening it, then, we need to think about how new forms of output will force us to revise our institutional structures, our forms of training and credentialing, our narratives of professional development, our models of research practice, our understandings of collaboration, and our forms of knowledge production, circulation and archiving.

Not all of the academic book's future users will be human. As machine-reading, text-mining, online 'social annotation' and related approaches come of age, the academic book will need to be optimised for new reading techniques. This creates particular challenges where the book includes non-textual content. As humanities researchers increasingly want to zoom in and out between 'distant' and 'close' reading protocols, the academic book will need to facilitate scaleable reading.[7] We must ensure that academic books are designed today in such a way that they will be findable, citeable and readable in the long term, using as yet undeveloped tools. Scholars in the future will want not only to write different kinds of books, but also to discover, study and interrogate books in new ways. The academic book of the future will need to be future-proof.

We can read printed books that are 600 years old. The academic book of the future may not remain useable for so long. The printed codex marries hardware (the paper and ink) and software (the words and ideas). This makes it one of the most durable data-storage technologies ever devised. This is not the case for electronic formats, where the 'content' needs to be readable on new devices powered by upgraded software. Most printed books exist relatively well in regimes of benign neglect. With reasonably constant temperature and humidity levels, and without overexposure to light or moisture, they remain readable for centuries.[8] The same is not true of electronic formats, which often become irrecoverable after only a few years due to obsolescent hardware and software. We therefore need to consider who will bear the ongoing responsibility and cost of maintaining long-term access and usability of academic books created in digital formats, and the datasets associated with them. This means remixing the division of labour that currently exists among faculty, publishers, and librarians.

As the academic book of the future takes shape, we will also need to engage seriously with the concerns raised in many quarters that digital media make sustained intellectual work more difficult, even while they facilitate research in some respects. Drawing on the neuroscience of reading, some commentators have asked whether the kind of long-form linear argumentation that has been the gold standard of humanistic scholarship will be sustainable in digital formats or will find readers among digital natives.[9] There is some evidence that reading on the screen produces lower levels of comprehension and retention compared with reading on the page, at least among the current generation of university students.[10] The kind of sustained absorptive reading the humanities value and academic monographs demand may simply be harder on screen, especially on internet-enabled devices with their endless potential for distraction.

Finally, there is a politics of the academic book. Those of us employed in the academy, especially in the UK, are increasingly asked to work faster, to submit to greater scrutiny, to be more responsive to agendas we didn't set, and to undertake research that will produce immediate, direct and measurable impacts beyond the academy. The academic monograph as a form, with its long gestation, its in-built reflection on its own working assumptions, its resistance to quick reading or easy summary and its aspiration to long-term significance, offers some resistance to these demands. The academic book of the future might allow us to work faster and more responsively thanks to the affordances of digital media. We must learn to benefit from these advantages, without accepting uncritically the managerialist insistence on accelerated production, the demand to be responsive and 'relevant', or the wider culture of endless distraction, soundbites and clickbait.

Scholars in the arts and humanities have already begun to reflect on how shifts in the media ecology will transform their work.[11] We now face the challenge of imagining how the academic book of the future will continue to make transformative contributions to knowledge. As new formats for the long-form output emerge, they have the potential to transform not only the way we disseminate our research but also the ways in which we conceive and produce it. Innovations from within arts and humanities scholarship and pressures from outside are combining to produce a shift in the forms of scholarly communication that may come to seem as significant as the introduction of print itself. Many people have a stake in the academic book of the future. If the UK can innovate in this area it will compete internationally for research talent, student recruitment and intellectual leadership. At the same time, we need to ensure that the most valuable qualities of the academic book as printed codex migrate to the new media environment without being devalued. If we get it right, new understandings of what a book can be will enable academic work that at present remains unwritten, indeed unthought.

Notes

1. Jerome McGann (1991) *The Textual Condition* (Princeton, NJ: Princeton University Press), p. 77.
2. See the report of the MLA Ad Hoc Committee on the Future of Scholarly Publishing: http://www.mla.org/resources/documents/issues_scholarly_pub/repview_future_pub, date accessed 10 September 2015.
3. Bonnie Mak (2011) *How the Page Matters* (Toronto, ON: University of Toronto Press).
4. Elizabeth Eisenstein (1980) *The Printing Press as an Agent of Change* (Cambridge: Cambridge University Press).
5. Chad Wellmon (2015) *Organizing Enlightenment: Information Overload and the Invention of the Modern Research University* (Baltimore, MD: Johns Hopkins University Press).
6. Lucien Febvre and Henri-Jean Martin (1976) *The Coming of the Book: The Impact of Printing, 1450–1850*, trans. D. Gerard (New York: Verso); Adrian Johns (2000) *The Nature of the Book: Print and Knowledge in the Making* (Chicago: University of Chicago Press).
7. See, e.g., Franco Moretti (2005) *Graphs, Maps, Trees: Abstract Models for a Literary History* (New York: Verso) and (2013) *Distant Reading* (New York: Verso).
8. An exception, of course, is books printed on acidic paper, which becomes brittle over time.
9. Nicholas Carr (2011) *The Shallows: What the Internet is Doing to Our Brains* (New York: Norton); Maryanne Wolf (2008) *Proust and the Squid: The Story and Science of the Reading Brain* (New York: HarperCollins).
10. Naomi Baron (2015) *Words Onscreen: The Fate of Reading in a Digital World* (Oxford: Oxford University Press).
11. Among many examples, see Andrew Piper (2012) *Book Was There: Reading in Electronic Times* (Chicago: University of Chicago Press); Matthew Kirschenbaum (2008) *Mechanisms: New Media and the Forensic Imagination* (Boston: MIT Press); and Marilyn Deegan and Kathryn Sutherland (2009) *Transferred Illusions: Digital Technology and the Forms of Print* (London: Ashgate).

Except where otherwise noted, this work is licensed under a Creative Commons Attribution 4.0 International License. To view a copy of this license, visit https://creativecommons.org/version4

OPEN

2
Wearable Books

Michael Pidd

Abstract: *This chapter explores a dystopian world in which technology has become pervasive throughout academic discourse, controlling the way in which books are authored, read, cited, and assessed. However, this is also a parody of the present: our obsession with data and metrics; our suspicion of consumer technology; and our unspoken feeling that there are perhaps too many academic books in the world. Above all else, this chapter seeks to reinforce the importance of books as the carriers of ideas.*

Keywords: digital humanities; ebooks; humanities; ideas; Linked Data; peer review; printed books; technology

Lyons, Rebecca E. and Samantha J. Rayner (eds).
The Academic Book of the Future. Basingstoke: Palgrave Macmillan, 2016. DOI: 10.1057/9781137595775.0007.

The Research Impact Framework of 2038 (RIF2038) was no more remarkable than previous RIFs in many respects. As a self-imposed audit of the impact of academic research by UK universities, it had been exhausting, expensive, hair-splitting, and largely ignored by the public for whom the Pub Enjoyment Index of 2031 remained a greater influence on undergraduate admissions. However, the RIF had become a bastion of the academic book in its wearable form. For those who pondered the future of academic books and, no less, the future of academic discourse itself, it was clear that unless the RIF changed its rules as to what constituted an acceptable submission (in other words, an acceptable catalyst of impact), Wearable Books were here to stay. RIF performance underpinned all promotions during each year's academic transfer window, so most scholars continued to spin Wearable Books without much questioning. Of course the fact that the RIF's rules were determined by the academics themselves, as they had been for time immemorial, tended to be forgotten by its critics.

However, dissenters of the Wearable Book did exist. It was not the specifically *wearable* aspect of the book that these people were unhappy with. There were plenty of media for accessing academic content, such as smart lenses that projected data onto the reverse of your eyelids, smart spectacles for the squeamish, and the electro-latex Data Projection Glove (reminiscent of surgical gloves) that pre-dated Apple's famous iGlove. Some people even accessed academic content on their television (unwearable books; because in those days the TV was connected to the Internet). Of course now we can easily summon sheets of interactive v-paper to appear thanks to the networked chip embedded in our hands. No, it was not the media that made Wearable Books alarming to some academics. It was the 'Linked Ideas' that underpin their content and the way in which these ideas were assessed.

It is perhaps difficult for many of us to recall that in the mid-2020s the use of Linked Ideas had emerged as the primary technical method for structuring academic discourse. It evolved from the earlier Linked Data concepts pioneered by Tim Berners-Lee, whereby structured information could be identified by computers, retrieved, and combined with other structured information in ways that were more meaningful for users. In other words, computers could appear to *understand* information. Initially Linked Ideas simply referred to a general set of technical methods for combining Linked Data, but the term gradually became associated with what happens when lots of information becomes dynamically linked together: ideas form. Eventually academics began authoring not only research data (in the sense of information) but also concepts, theories, beliefs, and opinions using Linked Ideas methods.

The result was a new type of book. Books were no longer lengthy discourses from the perspective of a single individual. Books became narratives that located, retrieved, and assembled ideas from all written discourse based on the topic at hand. For example, when reading *Bracknell Lives*, Snaghen and Bootmender's book about crime and poverty in late twentieth-century Bracknell, their ideas concerning the influence of human agency on Bracknell Forest Council's evolving social policy would be interweaved with the counter-arguments from Numen, Steer, and James, respectively. However, Numen's view that only call-centre staff exhibited agency in Bracknell would be counter-argued by Howie's reference to a data visualisation of TV-licence dodgers in Winkfield. The book would also give helpful tips where appropriate, such as 'people who agree with Snaghen also think this ...'. Readers would be led through a narrative that presented the tradition of argument and counter-argument. Readers were free to move on to the author's next idea once sufficiently illuminated or dulled by the present discourse.

Linked Ideas meant that the old distinction between articles, monographs, and co-authored books disappeared. Text was text. It was just a question of the length of an academic debate around an idea; the value of what was being said rather than how long it took for you to say it. Linked Ideas also enabled academic discourse and research data (the evidence on which academic ideas were founded) to be combined, enabling better scrutiny of one's interpretation of the evidence by others. During the early twenty-first century many academics had been peculiarly resistant to the idea of academic books moving into the same digital domains as their research data. Even ebooks were viewed with distrust. However, the rise of open content, the RIF, and the demise of academic print publishers[1] accelerated this change due to the citation effect that was created by the principle of 'if it ain't free then I ain't reading it'.

The beauty of Linked Ideas was that deliberately engineered academic algorithms were able to automatically identify, retrieve, and combine relevant aspects of other people's written discourse. Further, the algorithms would re-write the text in the process of assembling it, giving the illusion of a single-authored book without the discordance of different writing styles. Undertaking tedious literature reviews became a thing of the past, whilst those academics who failed to structure their books using

Linked Ideas methods would consign themselves to oblivion. Naturally, deliberately engineered academic tools had to be created that would assist with the process of authorship. These labour-saving tools would constantly scan an author's transcript and make suggestions as to where one idea began and ended, so that it could be tagged and identified as such. These helpful prompts were critical for ensuring that an academic's book was correctly tagged. You could switch them off if they proved too irritating, but that would be consigning yourself to oblivion. University libraries, who were the curators of Wearable Books, would never accept a treatise of unlinked ideas.

Linked Ideas enabled a revolution in peer review and assessment, subsequently adopted by the RIF. Academic peers were able to comment on a colleague's work instantly using the very same Linked Ideas methods and deliberately engineered academic tools. However, all responses had to be accompanied by a 'like' or a 'dislike' indicator for RIF counting purposes ('likometrics') because it was no longer considered practicable to actually read books for assessment. In the USA where academic books were driven by the tenure system, it was generally accepted that 1,200 'likes' were needed to secure a tenure, although these could be spread across multiple ideas, whilst 800 'likes' for an individual idea would promote it to the status of a fact and eligible for inclusion in *Wikipedia*. Since every 'like' had to be accompanied by a full, critical response to the academic's idea, and this in turn could be liked or disliked by other peers, computer science departments had been required to debate the minutiae of counting algorithms at length in published works that nobody ever read. Further, any ideas that received too many 'dislikes' would be relegated automatically by the algorithms. In other words, it was unlikely that a disliked idea would be incorporated into the discourse of a Wearable Book.

Wearable Books and Linked Ideas had originated in the sciences where lengthy discourse was not of interest, and had been developed in response to what had already been happening with popular fiction. Printed books were antique, the subject of book historians, and new books were only ever printed in paper or ebook formats as novelty gifts for Christmas and Father's Day. All useful printed books had been digitised and ingested into the universe of Linked Ideas long ago.

However, it was in the humanities that dissenting voices began to be heard, culminating in the RIF2038 when a university somewhere in Yorkshire included a printed monograph by the historian Professor

Audrey Chad as part of its submission. The subject of the book was unmemorable. It was unclear to the RIF panellists whether the book should be accepted or disqualified; whether they should count it or read it. Chad was asked if she would digitise the object and re-submit, but she declined to do so. Not even as an ebook.

As she would later say, 'It can be stultifying to be required to work within the constraints of the Wearable Book format, deafened by the constant noise of competing academic discourses that are the stock-in-trade for Linked Ideas, always reminding you that your own ideas are not an island'.[2]

In Chad's opinion there was sometimes a value in reading a lengthy, reflective work on a particular topic without the intrusion of other people's views; hearing a single voice articulating one person's ideas, irrespective of whether the ideas are transformative or not. This, she argued, was the genius of the old monograph in its printed form. Further, Chad argued that footnotes and a passing reference to primary sources could sometimes suffice, rather than blurring one person's discourse with the immediacy of evidence. 'Leave it in the repository! #StopTheData' she famously twerped.

Chad's book did little to influence the RIF, but it did give rise to Print Humanities and new ways of communicating research. It showed that non-digital methodologies can enable you to answer existing research questions from new perspectives, as well as explore new types of research questions that would be inconceivable using digital techniques. For example, writing slowly and at length could become a tool for thinking. Crucially, Print Humanities enabled academics to begin disempowering the class that sociologists now dub 'the knowledge elite': the people who understand how the technology of knowledge works, such as programmers, designers and engineers, as opposed to the consumers who simply use technology for access to knowledge, such as academics and others. Technology companies had been in the vanguard of this shift towards a knowledge elite in the early twenty-first century, but eventually even humanities scholars had need of a technologist in order to undertake research and publish their findings. Gradually – beginning with the transformation of the ebook into an unnecessarily over-complicated hypertext 'journey' – technologists dictated the shape of discourse.

Print Humanities is now emerging as a serious and respected body of methods within humanities research and communication. Practitioners have their own Manifesto. Barely a week goes by without a new Chair in Print Humanities being advertised, and the next RIF is expected to explicitly permit printed monographs, which will go a long way towards making printed books an acceptable part of the discourse ecosystem. The printed book's future is likely to be disruptive, with some academics declaring that it is here to stay and others believing that it will be a short-lived fad. Some colleagues even argue that Print Humanities should be treated as a new discipline. What is certain is that the future of the Wearable Book and Linked Ideas is no longer guaranteed. As such, a consortium of key stakeholders – academics, librarians, technologists and opticians – is now needed to explore what academic books might be like in the future.

Likes: 1,198. Dislikes: 7.

Notes

1. Most publishers merged with super-media companies to cash in on the trend for VR Fiction and the 'new novel' phenomenon.
2. Audrey Chad (2039) `Towards a Manifesto for Print Humanities'. In Tap and Spile (eds). *Proceedings of the Northern Powerhouse*. Yorkshire. Available for download in lens, spectacles, iGlove and TV formats. Click here.

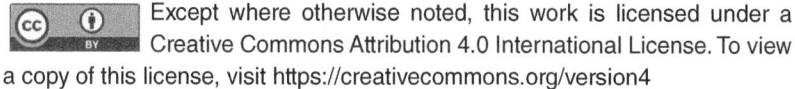 Except where otherwise noted, this work is licensed under a Creative Commons Attribution 4.0 International License. To view a copy of this license, visit https://creativecommons.org/version4

OPEN

3

The Impossible Constellation: Practice as Research as a Viable Alternative[1]

Sarah Barrow

Abstract: *This chapter draws attention to the features, values and debates of Practice as Research, arguing for its approaches, methods and outputs to be considered as equivalent to those used by more traditional humanities scholars, i.e. the 'academic book'. Indeed, it asks us to rethink our fetishisation of the physical book artefact as the pre-eminent model of publication in academic terms, and suggests we explore and support the development of other forms that might be more relevant to the digital age, and that attempt to break down the walls between theory and practice. It ends with a focus on the video essay form, which has the potential to reshape the subjects of Media and Film Studies in particular.*

Keywords: fetishisation of text; non-textual research outputs; Practice as Research; theory and practice; video essay

Lyons, Rebecca E. and Samantha J. Rayner (eds). *The Academic Book of the Future*. Basingstoke: Palgrave Macmillan, 2016. DOI: 10.1057/9781137595775.0008.

The difficulty with the term 'academic book' for those working in creative arts subjects, whether critical studies or creative production, or a fruitful combination of both these areas, is that the very word 'book' conjures up almost exclusively the image of a physical set of written, printed, illustrated sheets, made of ink, paper, parchment, or other materials, and fastened together at one side. And yet in an age of technical innovation, when we are encouraged by funders, institutions, our students and our own imaginations to think and work more creatively and to explore across traditional disciplinary boundaries, it is time to normalise alternative ways to publish and circulate ideas. This statement is not an attempt to undermine the enormous value of the physical 'book' or the rigour and review that goes with its publication; rather it is to do with seeking acknowledgement for and trust in alternative ways of doing and presenting research, valorising interdisciplinary and collaborative effort, and accepting that high-quality academic endeavour might result in something 'other'.

This brief essay highlights an approach to research and publication that has become increasingly important within the creative arts, and yet which still seems to be treated with scepticism by those more comfortable with traditional formats. This approach, most commonly known as 'Practice as Research' [PaR] has been much debated and scrutinised over the last two decades in particular, with a burgeoning literature, specialist subject networks, funded investigations in the UK and elsewhere, and a host of events that have attempted to gather together so-called traditional scholars with practitioner researchers to test the boundaries of acceptable research approaches and publication formats.[2] Since this approach emerged as a result of the establishment of positions, programmes, departments, and even universities of and for the arts when previously artist-scholars and art schools were regarded as separate entities, it has become necessary and desirable for distinctions to be identified between 'Practice as Research' and professional practice (whether from artistic or industry contexts) where the research element is not so vital. For Denis Nelson, for example, 'PaR involves a research project in which practice is a key method of inquiry and where, in respect of the arts, a practice (creative writing, dance, musical score/ performance, theatre/performance, visual exhibition, film, or other cultural practice) is submitted as substantial evidence of a research inquiry'.[3] It is a kind of 'practical knowing-in-doing', where insight, methodological rigour and originality are key, and might be shared with and learn from other practice-based disciplines such as education and ethnography. This issue for media subjects in particular in terms of the pre-eminent privileging of 'the book' was brought to the fore yet again in the most recent Research Excellence Framework 2014, when the sub-panel for Unit of Assessment 36 (Communication, Cultural and Media Studies, Library and Information Management)[4] failed to include a single practitioner-researcher.[5] This led to understandable anxiety amongst some academics (or their institutions) when it came to making the key decisions about which of their outputs to propose for submission. Many decided to play it safe and stick with the traditional output formats even when some of their most complex, rigorous and original work – with the most impact potential – had been produced in a media format: video, script, installation, sonic art, multimedia platform, for example. It is not just academic institutions that have been hesitant to support the Practice as Research approach, despite the possibility of embracing a more inclusive agenda in so doing. Within the media subjects, many professional practitioners-turned-academics from a more emphatically industrial background tend to resist the need to make explicit the specific research elements of their creative endeavour, viewing it as 'an unwarranted imposition from beyond their culture'.[6] Meanwhile, more established scholars in media with backgrounds in the humanities/social sciences have struggled to appreciate Practice as Research as a viable approach for subject areas that are still fighting to be taken seriously by the academy as disciplines in themselves. And yet, with increasing economic pressures, the need for practitioners, as Sullivan has put it, 'to consider their responsibilities as *researchers* as well as teachers' has become impossible to ignore and in fact has the potential to force institutional structures to open up 'in response to a new mood of innovation and change'.[7]

One PaR approach to enquiry and output that has long been familiar within the world of experimental media, and seems to be making a resurgence as a serious player on the research and publication agenda is the video essay/essay film. The term was used as far back as the 1940s by abstract Dadaist German film-maker Hans Richter, as a form that 'allows the film-maker to transgress the rules and parameters of the traditional documentary practice, granting the imagination with all its artistic potentiality free reign'.[8] During the period of the French New Wave (1959–68), philosopher film-makers such as Jean-Luc Godard,

Agnes Varda and Alain Resnais distinguished themselves with their 'interrogations of a world of images – and [...] the power of the moving image itself – characteristically set to literate voiceovers of wilful indeterminacy'.[9] The format continued to gain momentum and distinction amongst philosopher film-makers such as Chris Marker whose meditations on time, humanity and memory in *La Jetée* (1962) and *Sans soleil* (1982) are considered by academics and critics to be some of the greatest *film essays* (or, more accurately given their meditation on the nature of film itself, *essay films*) of all time. Indeed, the potential for cinema to become a vehicle for ideas about art and imagery, and about the world itself, has been acknowledged since at least as far back as the uber-film theorist André Bazin of the 1940s whose ontological approach to the image was part of an even older quest to 'secure the autonomy of film as both medium and art' that extends back almost as far as the birth of cinema itself.[10]

So, what is a video essay and how does it work as example of Practice as Research in terms of approach, genre and output that might be regarded as a viable alternative to the academic book? A substantial video essay, through both its content and its formal qualities, should of course provide new insights, whether into specific films or sets or films and/or into the aesthetic, socio-economic, political and/or cultural contexts within which those exist. The best of these might also break new ground in demonstrating how the emerging form of the video essay, often articulated as experimental documentary, without voice-over or subtitling, might help us to view the world from a fresh perspective. They should also, as Erlend Lavik argues, demonstrate 'the ability to not just engage with complex thought, but to pull it into focus, and to articulate and communicate those ideas clearly'.[11] Above all, the video essay should serve as 'a springboard to launch into a vital investigation of knowledge, art and culture in the 21st century, including the question of what role cinema itself might play in this critical project: articulating discontent with its own place in the world'.[12] The video essay format, which can vary considerably in length, has experienced a noticeable renaissance thanks to the work of respected theorist-practitioner-activists such as Catherine Grant and Michael Chanan, amongst others, who not only develop and distribute – mainly through peer-reviewed Open Access platforms – their own new insights through video-essay collections, but also champion the work of others in the field.[13] Indeed, for Grant,[14] the potential of the video essay is that it 'can inspire compelling work not only because, with its possibilities for direct audiovisual quotation, it can enhance the kinds of explanatory research that have always been carried out on films, but also precisely because of its potential for more "poetic", creative and *performative* critical approaches to moving image research.

Of course there will continue to be arguments put forward about the difficulties for the storage, conservation, referencing and archiving of such practice-led research outputs, as well as about equivalence with traditional outputs. The ephemerality and instability of such work, especially when dealing with performance or time-based multi-media installation, for example, 'pose particular challenges to the notion of a fixed, measurable and recordable knowledge'.[15] Nevertheless, the challenge must be taken on if we are to embrace the creative and epistemological potential of twenty-first-century technology; for, '[i]n the age of the digital, there is [surely] no need to stop, or even start, at the printed word any more'.[16] Let's hope that the main networks supporting the media subjects in the UK, MECCSA and BAFTSS will show leadership in this regard and support initiatives and opportunities for innovative routes to publication.[17]

Notes

1. Practice as Research is also known as Practice-led research and/or as Artistic research. These terms are not exactly interchangeable but are perhaps joined in that they share the overarching mission of the 'production of knowledge or philosophy in action'. See E. Barrett and B. Bolt (eds) (2007) *Practice as Research: Approaches to Creative Arts Enquiry* (London: I.B. Tauris), p. 5, where creative practice is situated within broader theoretical and research paradigms.
2. For useful bibliographies on this topic, see the references section in the edited collections by Nelson and Barret and Bolt. Most of the texts focus on performance and fine arts, and while many of the concepts, problems and approaches are transferable to media, I would argue that there is more work to be done on understanding the role of media industry professional practice in the academic research agenda.
3. R. Nelson (ed.) (2013) *Practice as Research in the Arts: Principles, Protocols, Pedagogies, Resistances* (Basingstoke: Palgrave Macmillan), p. 8.
4. HEFCE (2015) 'Expert Panels', http://www.ref.ac.uk/panels/, accessed 4 August 2015.

5 The chair of the main panel D, Professor Bruce Brown, is an inspirational proponent for PaR. However, sub-panel 36 included only traditional media theorists, archivists, librarians, former journalists, specialists in applied theory such as digital economy, creative industries and cultural tourism, and interdisciplinary work between arts, technology and the social sciences; no one engaged in the articulation and production of Practice as Research.
6 Nelson, *Practice as Research in the Arts*, p. 4.
7 G. Sullivan (2009) *Art Practice as Research: Inquiry in Visual Arts*, 2nd edn (London: Sage), p. xx.
8 H. Richter (1992) 'The Film Essay: A New Form of Documentary Film', in Christa Blümlinger and Constain Wuldd (eds), *Schreiben Bilder Sprechen: Texte zum essayistischen Film* (Wien: Sonderzahl), pp. 195–98. Translation by Richard Langston.
9 K. B. Lee (2014) 'Video Essay: The Essay Film – Some Thoughts of Discontent', *Sight and Sound*, http://www.bfi.org.uk/news-opinion/sight-sound-magazine/features/deep-focus/video-essay-essay-film-some-thoughts, accessed 15 August 2015.
10 A. Tracy et al. (2013) 'The Essay Film', *Sight and Sound*, http://www.bfi.org.uk/news-opinion/sight-sound-magazine/features/deep-focus/essay-film, accessed 15 August 2015.
11 E. Lavik (2012) 'The Video Essay: The Future of Academic Film and Television Criticism?' *Frames #1* http://framescinemajournal.com/article/the-video-essay-the-future/, accessed 17 August 2015.
12 Lee, 'Video Essay'.
13 Catherine Grant, for example, curates AUDIOVISUALCY: Videographic Film and Moving Image Studies, an online forum for video essays about films and moving image texts, film and moving image studies, and film theory: https://vimeo.com/groups/audiovisualcy. Another of Grant's projects is The Audiovisual Essay: Practice and Theory in Videographic Film and Moving Image Studies, intended to encourage further discussion and practice of this form.
14 C. Grant (2013) 'Déjà-Viewing? Videographic Experiments in Intertextual Film Studies', *Mediascape* (Winter), http://www.tft.ucla.edu/mediascape/Winter2013_DejaViewing.html, accessed 21 August 2015.
15 Nelson, *Practice as Research in the Arts*, p. 17.
16 J. Bresland (2010) 'On the Origin of the Video Essay', *TriQuarterly* 9(1), http://www.northwestern.edu/newscenter/stories/2013/07/the-video-essay-celebrating-an-exciting-new-literary-form.html#sthash.BpuwQbrG.dpuf, accessed 15 August 2015.
17 The MeCCSA Practice Network champions practice within the Media Communications and Cultural Studies Association, ensuring that those that

teach and research practice have a strong voice within the subject association and beyond. BAFTSS (the British Association for Film, TV and Screen Studies) has just launched the first Practice Research Award, reflecting the growing 'performative' tendency of film and moving-image research taking place in/through/around practice-based outputs.

Except where otherwise noted, this work is licensed under a Creative Commons Attribution 4.0 International License. To view a copy of this license, visit https://creativecommons.org/version4

Part II
Publishers

OPEN

4

The Academic Book of the Future and the Need to Break Boundaries

Jenny McCall and Amy Bourke-Waite

Abstract: *Market research demonstrates that scholars' attitudes towards monographs are changing, and that there is appetite for a shorter monograph form. The introduction of mid-length research format Palgrave Pivot in 2012 has proved that such a venture can be successful, and that more flexibility and speed may hold the key to the academic book of the future in humanities and social science research. In this chapter Jenny McCall, Global Head of Humanities at Palgrave Macmillan, and Amy Bourke-Waite, Senior Communications Manager at Palgrave Macmillan, consider the demand for Palgrave Pivot and similar mid-length offerings from academic publishers, the reception they have received from the academic community, and where we might go from here.*

Keywords: academic publishers; market research; mid-length offering; Palgrave Pivot; print on demand; publishing speed; shorter monograph form

Lyons, Rebecca E. and Samantha J. Rayner (eds).
The Academic Book of the Future. Basingstoke: Palgrave Macmillan, 2016. DOI: 10.1057/9781137595775.0010.

Traditional methods of publishing academic research, for scholars working in the humanities, business or social sciences, have been to choose to publish either one or more journal articles, or a monograph. Both follow standard formats which were originally dictated by the limits of printing presses. Most scholarly journal articles are between 7,000 and 8,000 words, and most scholarly print books are between 70,000 and 110,000 words in length, with little flexibility for any word count in between. Scholars whose research findings naturally falls in between those word counts have, for hundreds of years, either separated their long research into a number of journal articles (which requires a huge time commitment) or have expanded their word counts unnecessarily to fit the requirements of a monograph.

Reform of the status quo has been possible for a while. As sales of print monographs decline, digital publishing has been slowly on the increase. Journal publishing has embraced digital since the early 1990s, and sales of ebooks are growing, albeit slowly (according to analysts Simba,[1] they still only represent 6 per cent of sales). Meanwhile, print-on-demand technology has enabled publishers to run smaller print runs at increasingly lower cost and higher quality, further freeing content from the restraints of physical printing. In 2010, an article in *The Economist* claimed that 'About 10% of Cambridge University Press's sales of academic and professional titles are generated by books printed on demand – compared with 3% five years ago. Before POD, if sales of one of the publisher's books dropped below 50 copies a year, it was taken out of print. Now a publisher can keep titles available forever.'[2]

Emboldened by ad hoc conversations between Palgrave Macmillan editors and their authors, who seemed frustrated by having to adhere to what many saw as arbitrary boundaries set by the limits of traditional publishing and printing, in 2011 Palgrave carried out a programme of quantitative and qualitative research to understand how we might improve the academic publishing landscape.

The Palgrave Macmillan Research Panel was established in October 2011, and was formed of 1,268 researchers recruited from a wide range of disciplines and geographic locations across the humanities and social sciences (HSS). The in-house team devised and circulated a survey to comprehensively investigate the panel's views on the process of HSS publishing and specifically on the length of publishing formats. Of the responders, 93 per cent had published one or more peer-reviewed research article in the last five years, while 54 per cent had published a peer-reviewed monograph in the last five years.³

Two-thirds (64 per cent of the 870 who responded to the survey) felt that the length of journal articles was about right, while for monographs this figure was 50 per cent. The results demonstrated that a number of authors (36 per cent journal article authors and 50 per cent monograph authors) were not satisfied with the formats available to them. Almost all those who felt that the length was not right said that the length was too long. The results showed that only 16 per cent believed that current outputs (journal articles and monographs) were sufficient. Of those who felt that a mid-form was a good idea, or who were neutral, 84 per cent indicated that they would be likely to publish in this format.⁴

The survey responses confirmed the suspicion of the Palgrave Macmillan editors that for some members of the academic community, a lack of mid-length publication options and slow production times represented a real problem. A mid-length format for original research which published faster would represent a solution to that problem. However, the editorial standards our authors expected could not be compromised.

At this time, the mid-length research that was available consisted of condensed summaries of existing research. Springer, one of the bigger academic publishers, announced SpringerBriefs in November 2010. SpringerBriefs are concise summaries of cutting-edge research and practical applications across a wide spectrum of fields, usually between 50 and 125 pages in length. Springer produce versions in print, ebook, and MyCopy for readers to access 24 hours a day, and boast a quick turnaround for production.*

Similarly, Princeton Shorts were launched in 2011, an initiative by Princeton University Press. These were brief selections taken from previously published influential Princeton University Press books and produced exclusively in ebook format.⁵

Based on the market research we had undertaken, we believed that there was demand for high-quality, original, peer-reviewed content produced quickly. Consistently, participants expressed extreme dissatisfaction with the length of time it takes to produce a typical monograph. Many wanted to be able to publish research reacting to current affairs more quickly, especially in response to the Research Excellence Framework's request for academics to prove their works' impact.

The then Managing Director of Palgrave Macmillan Sam Burridge summed it up effectively when she told the *London Review of Books* blog: 'Original, cutting-edge research is the fire that fuels knowledge and education. Without the dissemination of new thought, new ideas, and challenges to current thinking, textbooks don't change, we don't learn from the past, and society doesn't advance. What we publish today will impact what our children study tomorrow, our social policy, and how businesses are run.'[6]

She added: 'Our role as a publisher now goes beyond the selection and dissemination of content. It's about ensuring the impact of research is at least equal to its importance. The humanities and social sciences find it much harder to be heard than the science subjects, as there is less funding and fewer tools available to support our academics. But we see our role as working to change this, breaking down boundaries, and in doing so, helping research to improve our world.'

Palgrave Pivots are a digital-first, peer-reviewed, original research format of around 30,000–50,000 words, with a commitment to publish the books within 12 weeks of acceptance. All elements of the Palgrave Macmillan publishing process were interrogated to allow for the mid-length format and enable faster publication. Authors are asked to answer any questions from copy-editors and typesetters very rapidly, and a wide range of attractive template cover designs are used instead of bespoke designs. In an interview with the *Vulpes Libris* blog, Ben Doyle, Commissioning Editor for Literature at Palgrave Macmillan, reinforced the integrity of the process. He said: 'All [Palgrave Pivots] are copy-edited and typeset by us and we certainly wouldn't expect authors to present camera-ready copy. Part of the service that we provide as a publisher is the layout/typesetting and editing... and we wouldn't dream of compromising on this to cut costs or to simply speed things up.'[7]

Print copies are available on demand. In order to ensure that the publication format would be used by academics in practice, Palgrave Macmillan liaised closely with stakeholders including librarians and booksellers to ensure that they would be promptly announced and correctly classified. The Higher Education Funding Council for England (HEFCE) confirmed that research outputs published with Palgrave Pivot are eligible for the UK's 2014 Research Excellence Framework (REF) – subject to all other criteria being met.[8]

October 2015 will be the third anniversary of the launch of Palgrave Pivot. In that time, we will have published over 550 books, which have taken an average of ten weeks to publish from acceptance. The shortest time to publication was Kath Woodward's *Sporting Times*, which was published in five weeks. The average page length is 132 pages, and the shortest 78 pages.

Palgrave Pivot titles are published by authors based at institutions all around the world, and they are already making an impact. For example, the Palgrave Pivot *Adoption: A Brief Social and Cultural History* by Peter Conn was published in January 2013 and cited in an Amicus Brief to the United States Supreme Court in opposition to Proposition 8, which would have restricted the recognition of marriage to same-sex couples. Conn would not have been published in time to influence the legislation if he had not chosen publish through Palgrave Pivot. Palgrave Pivot has been useful in accelerating academics' careers too. Sue Ellen Henry, author of *Children's Bodies in Schools*, wrote to her editor in August 2015 on the positive impact having written a Palgrave Pivot had on her tenure application. She said: 'I did get promoted (effective August) and while the committee doesn't give precise details about the review, I have to believe that having a book was a major supporting feature of my dossier. Indeed, I believe that one of my external reviewers learned of my book through the review process and then invited me to speak in a grad course via Skype on the topic.'

Ben Doyle described how Palgrave Pivot has changed the way he commissions: 'In terms of the kind of material that we've seen submitted for the format, the variety really has been surprising. I've published slightly more focused studies that require more room than a journal article affords but that couldn't be usefully padded out to monograph length. That said, I've also found the Pivot model to be a good length for particular types of work – work written in a more essayistic style, for instance, or work that adopts a more polemical tone. Many of the academics that I've discussed the format with have viewed it as an excellent length at which to make an initial intervention into an emergent area upon which other academics can then build.'[9]

Attitudes often change slowly in academia, and Palgrave Macmillan was prepared for adoption of the mid-length format to take some time. As Leonard Cassuto notes in his 2013 article for *The Chronicle of Higher Education*: 'The new, midsized kid on the block has a future, but […] it's not yet clear how long it will take to gain full welcome on the playground. Academe is conservative (with a small "c"). Such conservatism may guard against fads, but it may also slow change that can be necessary.'

Cassuto quoted one English professor at a state university who said: 'My sense would be that established scholars will have to give these new kinds of venues credibility first before more vulnerable younger ones can risk counting on them... That's just pragmatism speaking.' A dean interviewed by Cassuto speculated that tenure committees, deans and provosts would be 'more flexible than most might assume' but that 'the real conservatism on these questions comes from faculty who are afraid of looking too different from their peers'.[10]

However, Sam Burridge was amazed to see how academics reacted to the launch of Palgrave Pivot. She said: 'Authors have responded incredibly positively. In the 18 years I've been in publishing I've never been involved in a product with such a positive response... I don't normally get authors emailing me directly, praising us as a publisher.' The hundreds of books published since then attests to that.[11]

Recently, Goldsmiths University Press was launched in tandem with an invitation for academics to submit proposals for short or mid-length monographs, as well as short book and pamphlet series. Press director Sarah Kember told *The Bookseller* that the Press sought 'thought-in-action, provisional or process-capturing work' such as briefs, scripts, blogs, storyboards, notebooks, essays, clips, and previews.[12] It is also interested in non-standard modes and forms of communication, such as an article in the form of a comic or graphic novel.

Indeed, the market for mid-length research seems to be going from strength to strength. There are also now Stanford Briefs, an imprint from Stanford University Press, running at 20,000 to 40,000 words in length. They publish bite-sized original research in essay format, but aimed at a wider, more popular audience (as are Sage Swifts and Policy Press Shorts). In 2013, Palgrave Pivot introduced an Open Access option for authors who wish for their work to be freely accessible and shareable at point of publication. Much has been made, in the last few decades, of the potential 'death of the monograph',[13] but despite print sales declining recently, the slow but inexorable rise of digital and the influx of innovations such as mid-format research shows that the monograph still has life.

Notes

*As part of Macmillan Science and Education, in 2015 Palgrave Macmillan merged with Springer.

1. E. Newman (2014) *Simba Information Global Social Science and Humanities Publishing 2013–14*, http://www.simbainformation.com/Global-Social-Science-7935107/, accessed 8 October 2015, p. 26.
2. *The Economist* (25 February 2010) 'Just Press Print', http://www.economist.com/node/15580856, accessed 10 September 2015.
3. H. Newton (March 2013) 'Breaking Boundaries in Academic Publishing: Launching a New Format for Scholarly Research', *Insights* 26(1): 70–76.
4. Newton, 'Breaking Boundaries in Academic Publishing'.
5. Princeton University Press website, http://press.princeton.edu/titles/9803.html, accessed 21 August 2015.
6. S. Burridge (2013) '5 Minutes with Sam Burridge: "Palgrave Pivot is Liberating Scholarship from the Straitjacket of traditional Print-Based Formats and Business Models"', *LSE Review of Books*, http://blogs.lse.ac.uk/lsereviewofbooks/2013/10/28/palgrave-pivot-100-hours/, accessed 10 September 2015.
7. Vulpes Libris (2015) 'Palgrave Pivot: Mopping Up the Mid-Length Manuscripts', *Vulpes Libres* blog, https://vulpeslibris.wordpress.com/2015/04/29/palgrave-pivot-mopping-up-the-mid-length-manuscripts/, accessed 20 August 2015.
8. Newton, 'Breaking Boundaries in Academic Publishing'.
9. Vulpes Libris, 'Palgrave Pivot'.
10. L. Cassuto (12 August 2013) 'The Rise of the Mini-Monograph', *The Chronicle of Higher Education*, http://chronicle.com/article/The-Rise-of-the-Mini-Monograph/141007/, accessed 20 August 2015.
11. S. Burridge (2013) '5 Minutes with Sam Burridge'.
12. B. Page (30 July 2015) 'Goldsmiths to Launch "Inventive" University Press', *The Bookseller*, http://www.thebookseller.com/news/goldsmiths-launch-inventive-university-press-308334, accessed 20 August 2015.
13. J. Wolf Thomson (2002) 'The Death of the Scholarly Monograph in the Humanities? Citation Patterns in Literary Scholarship', *Libri* 52: 121–36.

Except where otherwise noted, this work is licensed under a Creative Commons Attribution 4.0 International License. To view a copy of this license, visit https://creativecommons.org/version4

OPEN

5

The Academic 'Book' of the Future and Its Function

Frances Pinter

Abstract: *Ripping off the physical covers of the 'book' and moving swiftly into the digital realm immediately raises a number of issues around form, substance, supply chains, delivery platforms, discoverability and business models. Heated ideological, philosophical, pedagogical, and political debates leave people either exhilarated or exhausted. The meaning of the word 'book' itself will never again be confined to that of a physical object to be held, admired, loved, subject to spilt coffee, or burning by dictators. The 'book' will be defined more around its function than any of its other characteristics. This chapter discusses some of the factors that need to be understood when pondering the new function of the 'book'.*

Keywords: book delivery devices; book intermediaries; book of the future; book supply chain; future of the book; knowledge infrastructures; monographs; publishing; scholarly academic books

Lyons, Rebecca E. and Samantha J. Rayner (eds).
The Academic Book of the Future. Basingstoke: Palgrave Macmillan, 2016. DOI: 10.1057/9781137595775.0011.

Any thoughts about this topic must first rip off the physical covers of the 'book' and move swiftly into the digital realm. This thinking immediately raises a number of issues around form, substance, supply chains, delivery platforms, and discoverability. Questions then spring up around business models. Thereafter, heated ideological, philosophical, pedagogical and political debates leave people either exhilarated or exhausted. One thing is clear though. The meaning of the word 'book' itself will change forever and will never again be confined to that of a physical object to be held, admired, loved, subject to spilt coffee or burning by dictators. The 'book' will be defined more around its function than any of its other characteristics.

Books have evolved alongside academic practices, which form an increasingly complex interdisciplinary web. These academic practices and realities have the potential to change with exponential speed, courtesy of digital technologies and knowledge infrastructures that are rushing (some would say struggling) to catch up.

The concept of 'knowledge infrastructures' is a useful lens through which to focus on this topic. Christine Borgman defines knowledge infrastructures as the 'ecology of people, practices, technologies, institutions, material objects and their relationships within each discipline'.[1] Publishers are part of this ecology. How are these infrastructures being transformed by the new digital affordances? What impact are these changes having on scholarly communications? And, what are the implications for the academic 'book'? Its function will be determined by where it finds itself located within these new infrastructures.

Whatever the new functions of the 'book' are to be, they will be influenced by the existing scaffolding around scholarly communications – as built up by publishers, libraries, intermediaries, funder requirements, tenure committees, and so on. The transition we are experiencing is taking place within a charged environment of conflicting and competing forces. Many are excited about these new digital affordances. But in reality, there are sunken investments in existing scaffolding within the ecology, entrenched interests in the status quo, and very real concerns about the varying speed at which good people who care about scholarship are able to adapt (or not) to the new world.

At a workshop convened by the Sloan Foundation,[2] participants agreed that some of the most salient features of the new knowledge infrastructures are that: '(1) borders of tacit knowledge and common ground are shifting; (2) complexities of sharing data across disciplines and domains are challenging but increasingly exciting, and (3) new norms for what counts as knowledge are being generated more quickly than ever.' These features, along with the opportunities opened up by computational interrogation of big data, are intertwined and contribute to defining the boundaries around the ecosystem of any subject area. This has profound implications for publishing.

'Scaffolding' may not appear at first glance to be the right term to describe the support role that publishers provide in a very fluid ecology. However, given the rigidity of the legacy systems of supply and delivery, it may not be a bad metaphor. Physical books that have sustained us so well for centuries were (and are still) served by a host of intermediaries including bookshops, library suppliers, and aggregators. In other words a vast, established supply chain exists that is no longer best suited to deliver the new 'book'. We are now experiencing a whole host of pressures that will require the dismantling and reconstruction of some kind of scaffolding. We are somewhere inside a fundamental transformation – in a 'pupal' stage of development. What will emerge is as yet unknown. Wherever and however we end up will be in response to changes to the way that academics conduct their work, how knowledge problems will be solved, and how traditional career paths might change.

What does all this mean for the 'book' of the future? Some of the challenges include: newly shaped ecologies of knowledge infrastructures demanding shared data; new forms of publication; interdisciplinarity; facilitated collaborative work; and fast turnaround. Features that are likely to remain are long-form publications, shorter narrative structures within a coherent whole that can stand alone (e.g. edited chapters) as well as collectively (edited volumes), alongside more sophisticated ways of presenting interpretation of data or sources in light of theory. Features of the 'book' that are likely to be less prevalent are the physical object (which may not be printed unless requested) and therefore 'writing' will become more influenced by the use and the embeddedness of multimedia. The rigidity of single disciplines will wane – though to what extent is still unknown. Digital affordances not only provide new answers to old questions – they encourage new questions to be asked.

For years, there has been tension between subject depth vs subject breadth. Interdisciplinarity too has always been controversial. Now, with new digital affordances, we no longer have silos of discipline-limited knowledge infrastructures. Nevertheless, the publishing industry (admittedly of necessity) has lagged behind, following an age-old inclination towards an obvious choice of bookshelf in an imagined bricks and mortar bookshop.

Publishers want their output to be more relevant to a wider market because there are now easier ways to reach readers via social media and digital marketing. However, to achieve this they need to create better metadata, think more carefully about what 'list building' means and work more collaboratively with authors as 'co-creators' of information about the 'book' as well as the content of the 'book'. The challenges in our new world for getting the provenance, metadata and ontologies right (essential to improving discoverability) is impacting on the new boundaries around the knowledge infrastructures.

We have not yet fully faced the implications of the basic infrastructural problem of metadata creation and maintenance, both from a technical and an ontological perspective. Nor have we fully grasped the huge benefits of metadata travelling with and within the 'book' rather than residing in an unattached catalogue. We don't have the metadata to facilitate building the bridges to create true interdisciplinarity. As categorisations in the digital world were built up from a single-discipline basis we don't yet have the standards demanded of our multi-faceted world. For instance, only now has a new universal and interdisciplinary coding structure called Thema come onto the market, transcending BISAC and BIC. Less and less fits into the traditional subject-based classifications of knowledge.

The challenge for publishers is to find ways of enabling these exciting developments to flourish. After that has been achieved, some kind of sense of the future 'book' will emerge. The 'book', depending on its function, will take its place within the ecology and support it. Its objective will still be to present complex arguments as well as synthesise existing and new knowledge in a form that is digestible to other academics and beyond.

Here is an attempt to identify just a few of the driving forces that will change what the 'book' will look like and its place in the world's knowledge infrastructure.

The monograph, long considered the gold standard, has a number of functions. First, it remains a rite of passage. Scholars who are looking for permanent appointments at universities need to publish a book (at least in the humanities and social sciences). This requirement may change in future – but not immediately. However, there are fewer permanent posts available even though universities are expanding.

A new career track is emerging sometimes referred to as 'Alt AC' (Alternative Academic Career) where researchers move from one short-term contract to another rather than joining an institution for the long haul. 'AltACers' may need to publish monographs for credentialing, but in many fields it may be that other forms of publication will suffice to launch their careers and demonstrate impact. They will have a plethora of formats and platforms available to them with which to disseminate their findings. The impact of their research will be measured by more than just citations. For recognition purposes the choice of medium will be important. This could result in fewer traditional monographs being published.

The 'cross-over book', for which publishers have always had high hopes, has its origins in the monograph. This well-written academic book that appeals to a slightly wider market – and most importantly crosses over into the book trade, stocked by upmarket bookshops and even reviewed in the national media – are few and far between. In reality those monographs that make it into paperback are usually bought by just a few hundred academics for whom the price is now acceptable for individual purchase (in either print or ebook format). There is scope for expansion here for as long as people still want their 'own' copy. Sometimes there is still a surprise success when a potential 'cross-over' book becomes a bestseller, as Harvard University Press experienced with Thomas Piketty's *Capitalism in the Twenty-First Century*.

It was in the seventies that American publishers recognised that there was money to be made from translating academic ideas into popular but serious books. Literary agents especially played a key role in coaching authors, explaining how to write for the general audience, how to build an 'arc' into the narrative, and so on. Some authors (and their agents and publishers) made a lot of money from this type of publication. Popular books in science and other subjects such as history are likely to persist so long as some people still turn to handy print introductions and overviews.

The 'enhanced ebook' is where attention is directed at the moment. But what is it exactly? A succinct definition comes from eBook Architects. 'enhanced ebooks' use enhancements that provide 'extras that make an ebook more interesting, informative, or interactive. They are also a way to add new content or functionality that would not be possible in the printed book.'[3] The term is used less now to denote simple links and covers a very broad spectrum, including audio-visual content.

It may actually be a website that contains long-form content that is not considered to be a book, but would be so in another context. The blend of text with other media offers limitless possibilities. However, it will be a long time before norms and standards are developed that make the 'enhanced ebook' into a recognisable commodity.

How knowledge infrastructures evolve will influence how enhancement facilities are used, and vice versa. Individual national requirements such as those of the Research Excellence Framework (REF) in the UK play a part in determining the kinds of outputs selected by researchers. The scaffolding needed to support dissemination should develop in tandem, but in reality is likely to move ahead in fits and starts.

Critically for different types of enhanced ebooks there will need to be better delivery systems and improved means of reaching the scholarly community. Peter Costanzo in a 2014 Digital Book World blog says: 'The main problem is that the market as it currently exists does not allow publishers to deliver the same enhanced product across all current digital platforms, whether it be Apple's iPad, Amazon's Kindle Fire, Barnes & Noble's Nook, and Kobo's Arc. And when you stop and think about it, no other content creator is faced with this conundrum.'[4] Delivery and delivery devices are still on the baby slopes.

The intermediaries that bridge publishers and libraries probably have a role to play in the new world, but their own business models need to adapt. As they consolidate through mergers there is the hope that this will lead to more investment in transitioning, facilitating experimentation and the shouldering of mistakes. On the other hand, there is understandable anxiety in the community that consolidation will lead to higher prices for libraries, squeezed margins for publishers and business models plagued with rigor mortis.

Discovery tools are improving, but have a long way to go. Another factor in this period of change is the open/tolled access divide: differences in who pays what, when and how have inevitably added a level of complexity to the next decade or so.

To conclude, much more is being demanded of the scaffolding than ever before. New business models, changes in the supply chain, improved metadata, and developments in better digital tools to help discovery and dissemination will all play a part in how the publishing community positions itself to serve scholarly communications. A definition of the academic 'book' of the future will be clearer after a further period of experimentation (length unknown) with what is possible. To date there are a number of initiatives coming out of university-based publishing, such as at Greenwich University. Some of these originated from libraries, such as UCL Press, while others have been spearheaded by the drive of single individuals (e.g. Open Book Publishers). New organisations such as Knowledge Unlatched are emerging to try new business models. All new approaches, however, struggle with legacy elements in the ecology. There is no single disrupter. Whether the functions of the 'book' will be executed by the most optimal and cost-effective publishing solutions remains an open question.

Notes

1. Christine Borgman (2015) *Big Data, Little Data, No Data* (Boston: MIT Press), p. 33.
2. Knowledge Infrastructures: Intellectual Frameworks and Research Challenges Report and Workshop, http://knowledgeinfrastructures.org/, accessed 15 August 2015.
3. Ebook Architects website, http://ebookarchitects.com/learn-about-ebooks/enhanced-ebooks/, accessed 15 August 2015.
4. Peter Costanzo (23 May 2014) 'The Real Reason Enhanced Ebooks Haven't Taken Off (Or, Evan Schnittman Was Right... for the Most Part)', *Digital Book World*, http://www.digitalbookworld.com/2014/the-real-reason-enhanced-ebooks-havent-taken-off-or-evan-schnittman-was-right-for-the-most-part/, accessed 15 August 2015.

Except where otherwise noted, this work is licensed under a Creative Commons Attribution 4.0 International License. To view a copy of this license, visit https://creativecommons.org/version4

OPEN

6

The University Press and the Academic Book of the Future

Anthony Cond

Abstract: *Long perceived as a bastion of the academic book, the university press now finds itself operating under a range of business models, in an increasing number of possible locations on campus, and with the measurement of 'success' markedly different across host institutions. Yet this study of the underpinning rationale for a growth in university press publishing in the UK, and of the award of major grants to several US presses, highlights that the university press remains a barometer for proposed structural changes to knowledge dissemination and debates around the future of the book in the academy.*

Keywords: digital publishing; humanities; monograph; Open Access; university press

Lyons, Rebecca E. and Samantha J. Rayner (eds).
The Academic Book of the Future. Basingstoke: Palgrave Macmillan, 2016. DOI: 10.1057/9781137595775.0012.

Much like the humanities field it so often serves, the university press has endured many decades of self-diagnosed crisis and introspective self-reflection. A report from the University of Chicago Press's Director in 1927 noted editorial and authorial concerns over such familiar issues as 'excessive specialization', and an inability to publish important scholarly work with small audiences.[1] This long-standing hand-wringing emerged, not least because of debates around the relative value – in library budget terms, among others – of humanities research, the outputs of which have frequently been that cornerstone of the university press publishing programme: the monograph. Thus the university press enjoys a peculiar position: a publishing island atop a sea of academia, its insecurities a mirror to the budgetary, utility and reputational concerns of the subjects and institution it serves.

One in six university presses now reports to a library.[2] Presses otherwise report to senior university managers or university or quasi-university committees; their editorial boards are drawn from faculty, yet more faculty are engaged as series editors, authors and reviewers, and more still in the inevitable exchange of ideas that happens when an academic department and a scholarly publisher active in its discipline are in close proximity. The university press is, thus, a touch point – above and beyond the author/purchaser/reader relationship with commercial publishers – between the academy's hopes and fears and the realities of the scholarly communication system, all the more so in recent years as savvy press directors have become more engaged in wider institutional politics in order to navigate institutional reorganisation. In thinking about the medium-term future of the academic book, changes in the university press landscape provide a tantalising glimpse of how a much written about soup of Open Access, digital scholarship, funding policies, authorial conservatism, challenging library budgets, publishing consolidation, internationalisation and new business models may be consumed.

In particular, a reading of the most recent round of grants from the Andrew W. Mellon Foundation gives an idea of how a future of the academic book is perceived by that great engine of scholarly book production, the membership of the Association of American University Presses (AAUP), who, according to the Association's website, collectively publish almost 15,000 books each year.[3] Whilst the 2015 annual conference of the AAUP provocatively included the panel 'When Publishers Aren't Getting It Done', the Mellon grants have provided much-needed capital for university presses to plan for the future. As Donald J Waters, Senior Programme Officer at the Foundation, has put it: 'University presses are seeking to retool their operations to take advantage of digital media and digital workflows to bring new works of scholarship to the broadest possible audiences at the lowest possible cost.'[4]

In May 2014, the Mellon Foundation sent university press directors a request for proposals for long-form digital publishing for the humanities. Noting the growth of digital scholarship, the Foundation recognised an 'urgent and compelling' need for university presses to publish and make digital work available to readers. It also recognised that it was challenging to find the resources that are needed to do so. The Foundation therefore asked university presses to submit collaborative bids to test new long-form digital publishing business models, or tackle its component parts, such as (1) editing; (2) clearing rights to images and multimedia content; (3) the interaction of the publication on the Web with primary sources and other related materials; (4) production; (5) pre- and post-publication peer review; (6) marketing; (7) distribution; and (8) maintenance and preservation of digital content.[5]

Projects that received funding from Mellon in response to this call, and in related funding immediately before and after it as 'part of Mellon's overall initiative in academic publishing', can be grouped into three broad categories: digital book platforms, Open Access tools and distribution channels, and platforms for enriching the user experience of books both before and after publication:[6]

- The University of North Carolina Press received $998,000 to develop a collaborative services platform for university presses, which will be used to facilitate cost efficiencies on a broad range of digital publishing activities, including copy-editing, composition, production, operations, and marketing services as part of the development of digital monographs.
- New York University Press, publisher of Kathleen Fitzpatrick's seminal *Planned Obsolescence: Publishing, Technology, and the Future of the Academy*, a book that has clearly influenced much of the thinking around the grant programme, received $786,000 to develop an infrastructure for enhanced networked monographs to support the editing, production, dissemination, and discovery of long-form digital publications in the humanities.

▶ University of Minnesota Press will work with CUNY's GC Digital Scholarship Lab to develop 'Manifold Scholarship', a project that will 'develop, alongside the print edition of a book, an alternate form of publication that is networked and iterative, on an interactive open-source platform'.[7] Ebook editions will allow authors to link to or incorporate rich media content, primary sources and datasets. Reader feedback – separate from peer review – will be incorporated via social media channels.

▶ The University of Michigan Press and partners at Indiana, Minnesota, Northwestern and Penn State, received grant money to build a hosted platform for managing monographic source materials and born digital publications. In practice, this means that an existing repository infrastructure will be 'extended to accommodate the interactive presentation of digital materials linked to humanities monographs through stable URLs and Digital Object Identifiers (DOIs) printed in paper versions and additional clickable links in electronic formats'.[8]

▶ The University of California Press and the California Digital Library will develop a web-based open-source content management system to support the publication of Open Access monographs in the humanities and social sciences. When complete, the system will be made available to other university presses and library publishers.[9]

▶ Johns Hopkins University Press received support from Mellon for the further development of that most successful example of University Press collaboration, Project Muse. MUSE Open will see Open Access monographs distributed globally and 'made visible and usable through discoverability and accessibility tools normally reserved for paid content' under the banner of one of the most trusted intermediaries.

▶ Stanford University Press has channelled its grant into establishing a robust peer review process for interactive scholarly research projects, including a system and framework for publishing and distributing digital-born scholarship.

▶ Yale University Press will establish a new electronic portal on which customisable art and architectural history content, drawn from Yale's backlist, will be made available to consumers and institutions.

▶ Although not strictly university press awards, the programme also gave $1.3million to Brown University[10] to support capacities at universities and presses for the development, publication, and preservation of born-digital interactive scholarly works, including a focus on the legitimisation of digital scholarship to ensure that digital and traditional scholarship are given equal credit in tenure and promotion; and $1million to West Virginia University for the development of Vega,[11] an online open sources academic publishing system that will support the peer review, copy-editing, and publication of multimedia-rich scholarship.

Is this, then, the direction of travel for the academic book of the future? In some cases certainly: it will be digital, it will be iterative, the cost of making it available in Open Access form (if so desired) will reduce through a shared infrastructure, it will be rich in supporting data, and the esteem of the university press brand and the rigour of university press peer review will be brought to bear on all of this. But it has been a mistake of a great many publishing commentators to pronounce on *the* future of the academic book when there is in fact no one future for it. Indeed, perhaps the sole common future of all kinds of academic book will be the process of credentialisation as being 'academic'.

According to a 2014 survey of 2231 academics undertaken by JISC,[12] 83 per cent of humanities scholars use electronic scholarly books but 87 per cent used a print copy for the last text they read. While percentages are no doubt in flux they point to an audience regularly imbibing scholarly research in more than one format, rather than an exclusively digital one. It is unlikely that the audience for print will disappear entirely. Intriguingly, of the 98 per cent of respondents who felt that reading the monograph was important or very important for career purposes only 10 per cent of respondents felt that it was difficult or very difficult to access monographs, which suggests that any significant growth in readership for the academic book in whatever form it takes will come from outside its conventional audience, regardless of new distribution strategies.

The practice of iterative publication, of utilising networked technologies and online communities, offers the potential for a deeper and more varied engagement from readers at different stages of the publication process. Research undertaken by Palgrave in 2014[13] showed that over two-thirds of the authors they surveyed thought publishers should be experimenting with alternative peer review methods: 'Responses indicated that rather than this interest being driven by dissatisfaction with existing peer review methods, it was inspired by curiosity in what new approaches might offer.' However, as Kathleen Fitzpatrick notes, 'even the most ingenious new structures for publishing a text online will not automatically get any randomly selected group talking. Technologies like these can, however, facilitate discussions among those who are both motivated and prepared to have them.'[14] The process will require careful curation to solicit engagement, requiring either a financial investment by publishers or one of time by authors, who, like their potential readers/reviewers already face the demands of teaching, research, 'knowledge exchange', conferences, writing and reviews of traditional scholarship, and so on.

The cost of long-form Open Access publishing will inevitably decrease through the welcome establishment of a robust, shared infrastructure, but it is still unlikely that processing charges associated with gold Open Access will drop to a level that is readily obtainable for the majority of academics, libraries and university departments without external funding. Much rides on the scalability of high-profile Open Access book initiatives such as Knowledge Unlatched, which piloted with a predominantly university press roster of publishers, and the nascent, Mellon-funded Open Library of the Humanities, which has mooted a books programme with a small group of university presses. The most rigorous assessment of Open Access business models to date, the *Monographs and Open Access* report led by Professor Geoffrey Crossick concluded: 'There is no single dominant emerging business model for supporting Open-Access publishing of monographs; a range of approaches will coexist for some time and it is unlikely that any single model will emerge as dominant.'[15]

Open Access monographs, then, will be an addition to, rather than substitution of, existing practice, and will be published under a range of models, but another thread of Open Access book publishing is also beginning to gain traction on both sides of the Atlantic: the textbook. In an age when the 'student experience' is king, with an increasingly diverse and international student body, and with teaching income the largest source of revenue for many institutions, the opportunity to develop bespoke Open Access e-textbooks, as is happening at the University of Liverpool – in a partnership between press and library – provides a real institutional benefit. Whilst this turn inwards in a future that is global may seem counter-intuitive, it is worth noting that the first fruits of the project will replace a textbook from a commercial publisher that costs £56 and has been a compulsory purchase for 900 students on campus each year. Indeed, JISC's wider project, The Institution as E-Textbook Publisher project seeks to ascertain whether the institution as e-textbook creator can 'help students by providing a more affordable higher education, and promote a better, more sustainable information environment for libraries, students and faculty'.[16]

UCL Press, another participant in the JISC project, is one of a raft of new UK university presses that have emerged in the last few years[17] unencumbered with legacy and with a forward-looking strategy. University College London, one of the largest and wealthiest UK higher education institutions, has been a public supporter of Open Access. Its new press is funded from the university's research budget, underpinned by a belief, following Kathleen Fitzpatrick, that universities should reassert their role in the scholarly dissemination workflow and outputs. Dissemination is UCL Press's goal and its measures of success are based on that idea, with the benefits of visibility for institutional research, wider use by policy makers and the hope of attracting academics and students to the institution as additional perceived benefits.[18]

In a similar vein, institutions from Goldsmiths to Cardiff, Westminster to Amherst College in the US have announced new university presses embracing Open Access, digital technology and a mixture of 'standard' and 'non-standard' forms of publication. Just as some universities were prompted by developments in digital printing to experiment with university press publishing, so Open Access and digital publishing has created a willingness in some institutions to invest not just in ownership of conventional publications but to create new kinds of publication that sit outside conventional silos.

It is worth reiterating that these new ventures, and the Mellon grants, are not the strategies and aspirations of publishers in isolation. By the nature of the university press, at some level there will have been input or approval or both from scholars, and often senior university managers and librarians. They show us that it is in the mix of publishing practicality and scholarly satisfaction or dissatisfaction with the current system that the future of the book lies. Where once hardback and paperback sufficed, a variety of formats developed in a variety of ways must be offered to continue the university press mission of supporting the dissemination of scholarship, for, as Joseph Esposito has observed, 'It's not what the presses preserve that is important but the work that they have yet to do. Universities invent the future, presses communicate those inventions to the world.'[19]

The signs so far are of a slow evolutionary branching rather than a radical revolution of the academic book. Its future is, above all, one of choice for author and reader alike. While the Mellon Foundation has hinted at further interventions, including possible pump-priming for an institutional sponsorship model, the academic book sits within a complex global web with many stakeholders and overnight change is unlikely. In preparing for a diverse future of the book, university presses would do well to heed the words of Rick Anderson: 'Libraries and patrons don't care if a publisher's strategy is innovative. Don't bet your future on innovation. Focus on increasing relevance.'[20]

Notes

1 Bean cited in A. Abbot (27 June 2008) 'Publication and the Future of Knowledge', Presentation to the Association of American University Presses, http://home.uchicago.edu/~aabbott/Papers/aaup.pdf, accessed 20 August 2015.
2 J. Howard (24 June 2013) 'For University Presses, a Time of Fixing Bridges, and Building New Ones', *The Chronicle of Higher Education*, http://chronicle.com/article/For-University-Presses-a-Time/139983/, accessed 20 August 2015.
3 See 'About the AAUP', *AAUP*, http://www.aaupnet.org/index.php, accessed 20 August 2015.
4 G. Mahalek (8 January 2015) 'The University of North Carolina Press Receives Major Grant from Mellon Foundation', *Publisher's Weekly*, http://www.publishersweekly.com/binary-data/NEWS_BRIEFS/attachment/000/000/6-1.pdf, accessed 20 August 2015.
5 Cited in C. Straumsheim (25 February 2015) 'Piecing Together Publishing', *Inside Higher Ed*, https://www.insidehighered.com/news/2015/02/25/researchers-university-press-directors-emboldened-mellon-foundation-interest, accessed 20 August 2015.
6 For more detail on the main awards use the links on the AAUP website: http://www.aaupnet.org/aaup-members/news-from-the-membership/collaborative-publishing-initiatives, accessed 20 August 2015.
7 University of Minnesota Press (20 April 2015) 'The University of Minnesota Press partners with CUNY's GC Digital Scholarship Lab to launch Manifold Scholarship – a platform for iterative, networked monographs – with grant from the Andrew W. Mellon Foundation', University of Minnesota Press website, https://www.upress.umn.edu/press/press-releases/manifold-scholarship, accessed 20 August 2015.

8 Michigan Publishing (April 2015) 'Building a Hosted Platform for Managing Monographic Source Materials and Born Digital Publications through Library/Press Collaboration', Michigan Publishing website, http://www.publishing.umich.edu/files/2015/04/Hydra_Fedora_Mellon_Proposal_Summary.pdf, accessed 20 August 2015.
9 R. Poynder (8 March 2015) 'The OA Interviews: Alison Mudditt, Director, University of California Press', *Open and Shut?* (blog), http://poynder.blogspot.com/2015/03/the-oa-interviews-alison-mudditt.html, accessed 20 August 2015.
10 C. Coelho (12 January 2015) 'Mellon Grant to Fund Digital Scholarship Initiative', Brown University website, https://news.brown.edu/articles/2015/01/digital, accessed 20 August 2015.
11 C. Ball (7 October 2014) 'Proposal to The Andrew W. Mellon Foundation', Dr. Cheryl E. Ball, *An Academic Portfolio*, http://ceball.com/wp-content/uploads/2015/01/PORTFOLIO-COPY-WEB.pdf, accessed 20 August 2015.
12 OAPEN-UK (2012) 'Survey of Use of Monographs by Academics – as Authors and Readers', OAPEN-UK, http://oapen-uk.jiscebooks.org/files/2012/02/OAPEN-UK-researcher-survey-final.pdf, accessed 20 August 2015.
13 H. Newton (28 February 2014) 'Experiment in Open Peer Review for Books Suggests Increased Fairness and Transparency in Feedback Process', *LSE Impact Blog*, http://blogs.lse.ac.uk/impactofsocialsciences/2014/02/28/palgrave-macmillan-open-peer-review-for-book-proposals/, accessed 20 August 2015.
14 K. Fitzpatrick (2011) *Planned Obsolescence: Publishing, Technology, and the Future of the Academy* (New York: New York University Press).
15 G. Crossick (2014) *Monographs and Open Access: A Report to HEFCE*, http://www.hefce.ac.uk/media/hefce/content/pubs/indirreports/2015/Monographs,and,open,access/2014_monographs.pdf, accessed 20 August 2015.
16 Jisc, 'Institution as e-textbook Publisher', Jisc Collections website, https://www.jisc-collections.ac.uk/Institution-as-E-textbook-Publisher/, accessed 20 August 2015.
17 A. Cond (18 August 2015) 'The University Press Is Back in Vogue', *The Bookseller* (blog), http://www.thebookseller.com/blogs/anthony-cond-309360, accessed 20 August 2015.
18 P. Ayris, E. McLaren, M. Moyle, C. Sharp and L. Speicher (2014) 'Open Access in UCL: A New Paradigm for London's Global University in Research Support', *Australian Academic & Research Libraries* 45(4): 282–95.
19 J. Esposito (7 March 2011) 'The New Economics of the University Press – A Report from the AAUP', *Scholarly Kitchen* (blog), http://scholarlykitchen.sspnet.org/2011/03/07/the-new-economics-of-the-university-press-a-report-from-the-aaup/, accessed 20 August 2015.

20 AAUP (2014) 'Library-Press Connections at the Charleston Conference', AAUP website, http://www.aaupnet.org/news-a-publications/aaup-publications/the-exchange/current-issue/1265-charleston-2014, accessed 20 August 2015.

Except where otherwise noted, this work is licensed under a Creative Commons Attribution 4.0 International License. To view a copy of this license, visit https://creativecommons.org/version4

Part III
Librarians

OPEN

7

National Libraries and Academic Books of the Future

Maja Maricevic

Abstract: *In the near future, national libraries could adopt new roles within the national research infrastructure, such as policy co-ordination, development of national and international interoperability standards, and improving the discovery of academic books, in addition to their traditional roles in ensuring long-term access and preservation. Equally, the complexity and resource-intensive nature of these changes, combined with the rising budgetary pressures faced by libraries, will mean that the future role of national libraries in scholarly ecosystems will depend on their capability to innovate and to transform their relationships with researchers, universities and research funders. This chapter considers some generic trends that might influence how national libraries engage with a growing debate about the future of academic books.*

Keywords: academic book; British Library; librarianship; monograph; national libraries; Open Access; preservation; research policy; scholarly communications

Lyons, Rebecca E. and Samantha J. Rayner (eds).
The Academic Book of the Future. Basingstoke: Palgrave Macmillan, 2016. DOI: 10.1057/9781137595775.0014.

National libraries provide essential research infrastructure for arts and humanities and social science researchers; they are national centres for academic books. Their traditional role of providing a systemic collection of national publications, in most cases supported by legal deposit (which in some instances has been in operation for centuries), creates comprehensive repositories of academic books past and present.

For many disciplines, national libraries offer an additional advantage of providing unique primary research sources, and significant international collections complementing a continuum of national academic publications. In such an immersive research environment, arts and humanities academic researchers in particular tend to become more than readers, and often develop a deep interest in, and understanding of, how national libraries acquire, provide access to and preserve their collections. In many cases national libraries' collections are seen as a resource integral to the future of their research. Some researchers spend many years investigating specific, often unique collections, while others expect national libraries to provide comprehensive resources for their discipline.[1]

Digital changes to date have not altered the essence of this close relationship between national libraries, researchers, and academic books. However, if academic books are changing, will this well-established relationship change in the process? Will national libraries become vast digital platforms, where the researchers of tomorrow can remotely manipulate text, data, and multimedia, producing new knowledge through digitally enabled collaborations? Or maybe such digital platforms will be created outside national libraries, emulating model of disciplinary repositories in sciences?[2]

It is difficult to tell if such integrated digital platforms will be appropriate to support arts and humanities research in the future. However, some present developments can help us to examine how national libraries, researchers, and academic books may relate to each other in the future.

Discussions about whether Open Access will be made mandatory for academic books by research funders are a useful starting point in examining how academic books might develop.[3] It is often in this context that we see most clearly that academic books are changing. Open Access debate has reinvigorated scholarly examination of research information policy and publication models in the arts and humanities.[4] The growing interest in Open Access has also led to experimentation with new acquisition, publication and dissemination models for academic books through pioneering projects such as OAPEN,[5] Knowledge Unlatched[6] and the emerging Open Library of Humanities.[7]

This does not mean that all changes in the academic book environment should be attributed to Open Access. A great deal of change is arising due to changes in researchers' reading and information-seeking behaviours as they take advantage of the pervasive convenience, immediacy, and speed of digital information environment.

In 2012 The British Library and Jisc completed a three-year longitudinal study of doctoral students, which followed a large cohort of 3,000 doctoral students and offered many insights into their research behaviours. For example, young researchers in the arts and humanities perceived ejournals as slightly more important than academic books, with nearly 30 per cent using Google as their main channel to find all resources they need.[8]

Another driver of change comes from the nature of academic books as a research output, alongside journal articles and data, which means that in order to remain relevant, academic books will most likely need to be 'rewired' to fit the same or similar research assessment environments, and to achieve wider and measurable impact through digital channels.

While we want to hold onto the distinctiveness of research communications in the arts and humanities, and especially acknowledge the unique role of monographs and other long-form publications,[9] we also need to acknowledge that some of the change drivers for academic books are similar to what we have already seen in the science, technical and medical (STM) publication environment. It makes sense therefore that we take a hard look at the changes that have taken place in STM and find out what can be learnt by all interested in academic books, including national libraries.

Looking at a recent report published by STM, the leading global trade association for academic and professional publishers, we see that technological innovation related to final publications is modest – it is usually a PDF of an article. However, there are significant levels of business process change – new aggregation models, new Open Access publication models, even new models of peer review. Another striking feature of STM publishing is the centrality of funders' mandates.[10] In this context, national libraries are acknowledged for their preservation role, and are placed alongside commercial preservation solutions such as CLOCSS/LOCKSS and PORTICO.[11] Significantly for this discussion, the report concludes that there is 'a growing focus on the researcher (as opposed to the library), driven partly by the redefining of the customer in the OA model, but also by a focus on research assessment and metrics.[12]

From the perspective of the national libraries, if academic books in the arts and humanities become more like ejournals, this would mean shifts in the expectations of arts and humanities researchers, including an expectation of universal remote paywall-free access for academic books.

The majority of academic books find their way into national libraries via legal deposit. In a digital environment, legal deposit for non-print works still makes this possible and it provides a long-term preservation solution for academic books, but it does not satisfy the researchers' growing need for immediate, remote access to digital resources.[13] Such access has to be provided through different mechanisms.

Typically, the access options can be extended by purchasing relevant subscriptions or through linking to Open Access resources, but both of these options require national libraries to find additional resources at the time of ongoing budget cuts for libraries in many countries. As funding becomes more constrained, it becomes harder for national libraries to make a case for required investments in scholarly publications, while also developing their capability to manage the multitude of other digital publications – non-academic ebooks, online newspapers, growing audio and video collections, web archives, and digitised heritage collections. For many of these collections national libraries may be the only home, while the higher education sector has a well-developed library infrastructure and possibly a greater incentive to invest in academic digital resources. In today's resource-constrained environment, it could be argued that arts and humanities research would be better served by national libraries if they focused more on digital collections outside scholarly publishing, which are also essential in arts and humanities research.

Following and adjusting to the complexity of changes in research environments is an expensive and resource-demanding undertaking. Changes in scholarly communications are usually bespoke and follow the rules of research process as much as that of digital publication. Understanding this changing environment means constantly maintaining and growing the capacity to understand academic research, which requires appropriate funding and expertise. National libraries aiming to remain a relevant home for academic books in the future need to consider both their appetite and readiness to meet the changes taking place in arts and humanities research and academic books publication.

We should not be surprised if, under these conditions, a legitimate outcome for national libraries becomes less of a focus on academic books. Inevitably this will mean that the role of the national library as an integrated arts and humanities research ecosystem could be altered and reduced, which is why it is much more likely that national libraries will want to continue their long involvement with academic books – including both their preservation and improving access for researchers. This will be even more likely if it is clear that this continues to be important to researchers in arts and humanities.

The British Library holds 14.7 million monographs, and in 2013/14 alone added 107,554 through legal deposit.[14] For this collection to grow and to remain relevant in the future, it is essential for the British Library to understand and anticipate the changes in the academic publishing environment and to work closely with others to meet the challenges of rising costs and the increasing complexity of digital processes.

On this journey it will be essential for national libraries to strengthen relationships with the parts of government that have responsibility for research policy and research funding. Again, looking at the Open Access developments to date,[15] it is noticeable that national libraries play a more prominent role in the Open Access implementation in those countries where there are strong links between research funders and national libraries. A description of such a relationship in Sweden paints a picture of a national library as 'a catalyst for a closer cooperation between the main bodies of research and research libraries in advancing an open access agenda and developing a digital research information infrastructure'.[16]

This points to another key set of relationships that needs to be in place, with academic libraries more generally. In the UK a key document describing the need for closer collaboration of policy-makers, academic libraries, and national libraries is *A National Monograph Strategy* published in 2014. It is interesting that this document recognises the need for collaboration in the digital environment, but it also highlights the need for collaborating in improving management of existing physical collections, which is important if the future arts and humanities publication landscape is to retain physical books.[17]

One of the most significant alliances with academic libraries should be around the common understanding of the importance of digital preservation. For instance, recent research undertaken in academic libraries and repositories shows the difficulties that they face in maintaining, preserving, and providing long-term access to ebook collections.[18] It is an additional reason why preservation of academic books should remain at the centre of future considerations in national libraries.

The British Library worked with the Research Councils UK and the Global Research Council in April 2015 to examine the current status of policy and practice in Open Access communications. This forum reported the following in relation to preservation:

> Libraries can play a key role here: the current system of legal deposit libraries is effective in picking up most research to be curated and preserved for the long-term. This is a mix of physical and digital at the moment, but is moving towards predominantly digital deposit. However, as the legal deposit system only picks up published material in each national domain that has such provision, we need to think about new models of long-term archiving and preservation for OA materials that are being made available outside traditional publishing.[19]

While the national libraries' eye on future preservation issues is essential, it is also important that they experiment with emerging possibilities for access and use of digital scholarly content. If the academic book of the future becomes a flexible, engaging digital object, this may enable national libraries to provide new services not only to academic researchers, but also to their public and business audiences. The most effective way of finding what these future uses might look like is by allowing room for experimentation.

One such experiment is the recent BL Lab[20] project, which digitally 'cut out' one million images from nineteenth-century books, mostly monographs, and placed them on Flickr. To date these images have been viewed 271 million times and the public has added 422,000 tags to these images. In the process, the British Library learned a lot about crowdsourcing and about the potential for re-use of book images and illustrations.[21] Another such activity was producing the British Library's first MOOC in collaboration with the University of Nottingham – *Propaganda and Ideology in Everyday Life*. This digital course contains a series of videos, texts, collection show-and-tells, and interactive discussions. Would the academic book of the future be doing something similar? Will it become a collection of different digital elements combined to expound a long-form academic argument?

We do not know yet. However, a national library that is open to exploring these new formats will be in a better place to consider changing formats of publication in the future. The British Library's collaboration with the AHRC to develop the research call for The Academic Book of the Future project, and its subsequent work with the project research team and other stakeholders encapsulates what might be needed right now: a research funder and a national library collaborating to find new insights from research communities, and in the process engaging with wider researcher communities, libraries, and publishers to discuss issues that we have hitherto been considering separately from each other.

The present moment offers an exciting environment for experimentation, for building new and deepening existing relationships, which in turn may lead to a common understanding of what we want the academic books of the future to do – if we want them to be different, in which ways, and to what purpose.

Notes

1   In December 2011 The British Library surveyed nearly 3,000 academic researchers of whom 43.8 per cent said that they would have not achieved all their research aims without The British Library's collections. These researchers rated highly The British Library's capability to provide both the breadth and depth of content that supports their research across a wide range of disciplines. The survey data has not been published. Few respondents' views (Shelagh Rowan-Legg, Diana Newall and Alex Hall) were recorded for the Made with the British Library campaign: http://www.bl.uk/made-with-the-british-library, accessed 5 September 2015.
2   PubMed http://www.ncbi.nlm.nih.gov/pubmed and Europe PubMed Central https://europepmc.org – disciplinary repositories and discovery platforms that bring together biomedical literature including life science journals and online books, accessed 5 September 2015.
3   The majority of public research funders in Europe and around the world, as well as an increasing number of independent and charity research funders, now mandate that the outputs of research that they fund should be made available free of charge to end users, with the cost being met elsewhere in the publication process. The majority of such mandates focus on journals and do not include academic books, but this remains a developing agenda. The future mandate for Open Access might include academic books. For example, a recommendation to consider an Open

Access mandate for scholarly monographs is given in a report produced by Sir Bob Burgess for the Research Councils UK – *Review of the Implementation of the RCUK Policy on Open Access* (2015): http://www.rcuk.ac.uk/research/openaccess/2014review/, accessed 10 September 2015.

4   Prominent UK examples include G. Crossick (2014) *Monographs and Open Access: A Report to HEFCE*, http://www.hefce.ac.uk/media/hefce/content/pubs/indirreports/2015/Monographs,and,open,access/2014_monographs.pdf, accessed 20 August 2015, and a collection of essays edited by Nigel Vincent and Chris Wickham (2013) *Debating Open Access* (London: British Academy).

5   See http://www.oapen.org/home, accessed 5 September 2015.

6   See http://www.knowledgeunlatched.org, accessed 5 September 2015.

7   See https://www.openlibhums.org, accessed 5 September 2015.

8   *Researchers of Tomorrow: The Research Behaviour of Generation Y Doctoral Students* (2012) (London, British Library and Jisc).

9   Crossick, *Monographs and Open Access*.

10 M. Ware and M. Mabe (2015) *The STM Report – An Overview of Scientific and Scholarly Journal Publishing*, 4th edn (STM, International Association of Scientific, Technical and Medical Publishers).

11 Ware and Mabe, *The STM Report*, p. 31.

12 Ware and Mabe, *The STM Report*, p. 159.

13 In the UK the legal deposit of non-print works allows legal deposit libraries to receive digital publications from the UK for preservation, with some exceptions. They can provide access to this material only in their buildings, and only for one reader at the time. For detail see 'The Legal Deposit Libraries (Non-Print Works) Regulations' (2013) http://www.legislation.gov.uk/uksi/2013/777/pdfs/uksi_20130777_en.pdf, accessed 5 September 2015.

14 'British Library Annual Report and Accounts 2013–14', http://www.bl.uk/aboutus/annrep/2013to2014/annual-report2013–14.pdf, accessed 10 September 2015.

15 Open Access policies tend to be developed incrementally in order to maintain stability of scholarly communication, control costs and ensure flexibility to adapt to new digital developments. These developments typically include consultative processes with different stakeholders such as research funders, publishers, universities and libraries, including national libraries. In the UK, Universities UK are currently managing such a stakeholder group, monitoring implementation of Open Access policies.

16 J. Hagerlid (2011) 'The Role of the National Library as a Catalyst for an Open Access Agenda: The Experience of Sweden', *Interlending and Document Supply*, 39(2): 115–18

17 B. Showers (2014) *A National Monograph Strategy*, http://monographs.jiscinvolve.org/wp/, accessed 10 September 2015.

18 E. Collins and G. Stone (2014) 'Open Access Monographs and the Role of the Library', *Insights – OA Monograph Supplement*, 11–16.
19 RCUK (2015) 'Unlocking the Future: Open Access Communication in a Global Research Environment', *RCUK website*, http://www.rcuk.ac.uk/media/announcements/150527/, accessed 10 September 2015.
20 See http://labs.bl.uk, accessed 5 September 2015.
21 This British Library blog describes how these images have been used by the Burning Man festival: http://www.bl.uk/events/crossroads-of-curiosity-the-british-library-meets-burning-man, accessed 5 September 2015.

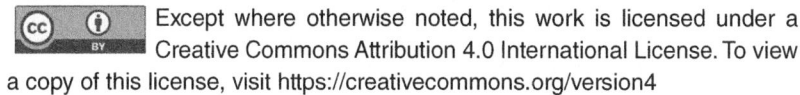 Except where otherwise noted, this work is licensed under a Creative Commons Attribution 4.0 International License. To view a copy of this license, visit https://creativecommons.org/version4

OPEN

8

Strategic Engagement and Librarians

Neil Smyth

Abstract: *The future of the academic book is a strategic engagement issue for librarians. Books might not be stored in or purchased for university libraries; they might not even exist in a physical form. How will academic books be organised and accessed in the future, if they are not in libraries? How will librarians at universities engage academic researchers in strategic conversations about the future of their academic books? This chapter argues that conversations between librarians and academic book authors about the future are more important than ever. It puts the current challenges in context, using data from the Research Excellence Framework and the University of Nottingham library catalogue, identifying the strategic role of librarians in shaping the future of the academic book through strategic engagement.*

Keywords: ebooks; JSTOR; library data; Open Access; relationship management; Research Excellence Framework (REF); strategic engagement; UK Research Reserve

Lyons, Rebecca E. and Samantha J. Rayner (eds).
The Academic Book of the Future. Basingstoke: Palgrave Macmillan, 2016. DOI: 10.1057/9781137595775.0015.

Academic books are those books used by academics in their research, and those books written as a result of academic research. While academics write books and prepare reading strategies for students, librarians develop systems, services and infrastructure for organising knowledge. But how do librarians engage academics in conversations about the future of academic books? This chapter examines the relationship between librarians and academic authors. It puts the current challenges into context, using data from the recent Research Excellence Framework (REF) and the University of Nottingham library catalogue, and identifies the role of librarians in shaping the future of the academic book through strategic engagement.

Challenges with the academic book have existed for a long time. While Vice-Chancellor at the University of Nottingham, Colin Campbell spoke about the future of scholarly communication. He described the library as his 'laboratory', but also highlighted some important issues: greater numbers of books are being published; student demands are increasing; academics increasingly require specialist material – to name but a few. Through all of these challenges 'the library is emotionally important to academics and vital to the well-being of any University'.[1] Open Access promised reductions in the cost of subscriptions, but fees are adding to the 'total cost of publication' for journals.[2] It is obvious that if libraries are spending more money on expensive journal subscriptions, there is less money available for books. This puts further pressure on funds that could otherwise be invested in academic books.

Academic publishing has been described as a Wild West,[3] but it is undeniable that long-form publications are important.[4] Some monographs have been described as literary[5] or 'semi-popular'.[6] During early conversations about the SOFT (Sprinting to the Open FuTure) project at Nottingham, which is part of the wider Academic Book of the Future project, literary outputs were identified as important. The REF is a key factor, as there may be a correlation between monographs and a four-star rating, creating a strategic university interest in some academic books. If academic books continue to be important to the REF and funding, it is more important than ever before to consider the place of libraries in this process.

Perhaps the most sensitive issue in the relationship between academic and librarian is the removal of books and other research materials from the library space. There are high expectations for many academics with regard to library holdings, and an even higher expectation that their own authored books will be in the university library. Although printed books are being removed from libraries – to create new research reading spaces, for example – they will undoubtedly continue to be in university libraries for a long time. A review of the arts and humanities Authored Books submitted to the REF by the University of Nottingham in 2014 showed that 92 per cent were purchased by the university library, and over 90 per cent were purchased in printed format.

Consider the removal of journals from libraries. JSTOR has been publicly available since 1997.[7] In 2012 the University of Nottingham removed most of the arts and humanities printed journals in libraries that were available through JSTOR. There were no objections from academic staff because of conversations over many years and the high level of confidence and trust in JSTOR. Many universities, however, continue to have printed journals on shelves when there is a trusted electronic alternative. The UK Research Reserve (UKRR) was created to de-duplicate journals and release shelf space but it may be extended to monographs.[8] A focus on the UKRR out of scope materials, such as superseded editions of teaching materials, popular fiction, indexes and newspapers, will allow more time for conversations about the more contentious academic books. For many librarians the academic book of the future will be managed as part of wider, national and international 'conscious coordination'.[9] There is a need for conversations about long-term planning and this will involve challenges, but it is arguably the ongoing conversation that is important.

There is growing investment in ebooks to improve student access, particularly through new publishing initiatives such as Demand Driven Acquisition and Evidenced Based Acquisition, or by providing free core readings in e-textbook form to first year undergraduate students.[10] Of the Authored Books submitted to the REF at the University of Nottingham, however, 40 per cent were bought as ebooks and 21 per cent as both print and ebooks, with just 3 per cent as electronic only. These ebooks still tend to look like familiar printed books, but there will be new forms of digital academic book that are not skeuomorphic.[11] It seems that for now and in the short term, only a small number of academic books will be available exclusively as ebooks.

Perhaps ebooks do not fit with all research and reading needs. They have been described as one more example of 'content that never contents'.[12] Some academics report negative experiences using ebooks, terming them as 'nerve-wrecking' and 'an absolute pain'. They have claimed that 'no one wants to read the d****d things' and lamented, 'it depresses me more than I can say that we can buy electronic resources seemingly without end but not books'.[13] Librarians have an important role in bridging the digital divide.[14] Some university libraries are now providing combined 3D printing and 3D scanning services.[15] If there are preferences for reading print, new print services may emerge. Libraries may offer services based on printing whole academic books that are available online, flipping the traditional library-service development: instead of print to digital, digital to print. More than ever it is essential for librarians to talk with academics about their own research reading, and reading expectations for students, as well as with publishers about the ongoing development of new platforms and new formats for different forms of academic book.

There is an increasing need to put academic authors at the heart of libraries and to consider students as future academic book authors.[16] If our students, the authors of the future, are to write sustained arguments over 80,000–100,000 words, they will need to read arguments of this length. The library is academic-led and library-administered. It is driven by what academics read and write, and by research and publication strategies – so it is important that they are involved with their university library. The arts and humanities collection in the Hallward Library at the University of Nottingham, for example, has more than one book by an academic author who works within half a mile of the library on almost every shelf. Yet there are some authors who never visit the library, even when they live in close proximity. How can this be addressed? One idea is using shelf-end signs with images of book covers or the photographs of authors as Aestheticodes,[17] linking to films of academic authors talking about their books. In this scenario, authors appear when you browse the shelves, reading from the book or talking about the book. Making the physical library connect with the digital library might be one way to inspire students to write the academic books of the future.

Librarians are moving towards new forms of scholarly relationship management.[18] Bains has described the change to a functional structure with separate research and academic engagement teams in one university library.[19] Working in this changing environment is about keeping an agile mind open to many possible alternative futures, and adapting to thrive in whatever new conditions arise.[20] Kenny has articulated the challenge:

DOI: 10.1057/9781137595775.0015

Can library liaisons play a key role in revitalizing human-to-human interactions by engaging individuals collectively in problem solving, creativity, and the production of new knowledge and awareness? Can the library become the center for engagement on campus, with liaisons providing critical human support and analysis that cuts across technology, disciplines, hierarchies, social norms, and institutional and cultural contexts?[21]

For many librarians in recent years, Open Access has been the basis for strategic engagement. Librarians have been 'leading change' in scholarly communication as 'positional leaders' and have been 'an active part of the academic life on campus'.[22] Some have developed strategies for 'relational communications'[23] and Scholarly Conversations[24] or used Open Access ACCESS week 'to provide leadership on campuses concerning scholarly communications'.[25] Changes and adjustments to policies[26] provide further opportunities for conversations. There is likely to be a high level of compliance with the HEFCE policy for Open Access journals and conference proceedings. Although no submitted Authored Books were available in Nottingham ePrints at the last REF, Nottingham authored monographs are becoming available through Open Access,[27] and it is likely that many more will be deposited in UK institutional repositories before REF 2026. One of the challenges for libraries will be integrating Open Access outputs with the indexed content in discovery systems. There is an opportunity for senior academic engagement librarians to focus on strategic and influential faculty conversations, including: the future of the academic book; changing publisher policies; licensing and third-party copyright; and new forms – from Open Access monographs to nanopublications and research data connected to books.

Working with academic authors is not always smooth, straightforward or easy. There is a need for collaboration.[28] Silver, for example, described how the Authors@UF programme enabled librarians to exercise this new role of outreach and engagement by working directly with faculty scholars to present his or her research, making the library the heart of interaction and strategic engagement.[29] However, librarians need support. Posner identified some of the common challenges and complexity facing librarians collaborating and engaging with academics.[30]

Librarians have a key role in shaping the future of the academic book through strategic engagement with the academic community. More importantly, though, this involves placing academic authors at the heart of libraries and considering students as the authors of the future. We need to better understand how strategic conversations can be effective in shaping digital scholarship and the future of scholarly communication. The AHRC/British Library Academic Book of the Future Project, and this volume of essays, generated by some of those conversations, show how complex and rewarding such collaborations can be.

Notes

1. C. Campbell (J1990) 'The Future of Scholarly Communication', in K. Brookfield (ed.) *Scholarly Communication and Serials Prices: Proceedings of a Conference Sponsored by The Standing Conference of National and University Libraries and The British Library Research and Development Department* (London: Bowker-Saur), pp. 11–13
2. S. Pinfield, J. Salter, P. A. Peter and A. Bath (2015) 'The "Total Cost of Publication" in a Hybrid Open-Access Environment: Institutional Approaches to Funding Journal Article-Processing Charges in Combination with Subscriptions', *Journal of the Association for Information Science and Technology*, http://onlinelibrary.wiley.com/doi/10.1002/asi.23446/epdf, accessed 25 August 2015.
3. C. Lambert (2015) 'The "Wild West" of Academic Publishing: The Troubled Present and Promising Future of Scholarly Communication', *Harvard Magazine*, http://harvardmagazine.com/2015/01/the-wild-west-of-academic-publishing, accessed 25 August 2015.
4. G. Mock (2013) 'Surprising Bright Future for Academic Books', *Duke Today*, https://today.duke.edu/2013/12/dukepress, accessed 25 August 2015.
5. The University of Nottingham's REF submission included two novels by Jon McGregor: *Even the Dogs* (2010) and *This Isn't the Sort of Thing that Happens to Someone Like You* (2013). There was also a collection of poetry by by Matthew Welton: *We needed coffee but...* (2009).
6. The Analysis of Research Excellence Framework Submitted Outputs for the Arts and Humanities at the University of Nottingham highlighted examples of academic books that were not submitted to the REF. For instance, in addition to four publications for the Research Excellence Framework, Professor Stephen Mumford, Dean of the Faculty of Arts at the University of Nottingham, published two very short introductions to causation and metaphysics with Oxford University Press and a book about sport: *Watching Sport: Aesthetics, Ethics and Emotion.*
7. R. C. Schonfeld (2003) *JSTOR: A History* (Princeton, NJ: Princeton University Press), p. xvi.
8. D. Yang (2013) 'UK Research Reserve: A Sustainable Model from Print to E?', *Library Management*, 34(4/5): 309–23.

9 B. Lavoie and C. Malpas (2015) *Stewardship of the Evolving Scholarly Record: From the Invisible Hand to Conscious Coordination* (Dublin, Ohio: OCLC Research), http://www.oclc.org/content/dam/research/publications/2015/oclcresearch-esr-stewardship-2015.pdf, accessed 25 August 2015.

10 T. Dickinson (2015) 'Free Core E-Textbooks: A Practical Way to Support Students', http://www.cilip.org.uk/cilip/blog/free-core-e-textbooks-practical-way-support-students, accessed 25 August 2015.

11 T. Abba (2013) 'The Future of the Book Shouldn't Be Skeuomorphic', *New Statesman*, http://www.newstatesman.com/culture/2013/02/future-book-shouldnt-be-skeuomorphic, accessed 25 August 2015.

12 K. Webb (17 July 2015) 'The Content that Never Contents', *Times Literary Supplement*, p. 19.

13 Examples taken from recent correspondence with academic book authors at the University of Nottingham.

14 A. Seyed Vahid and M. Alireza Isfandyari (2008) 'Bridging the Digital Divide: The Role of Librarians and Information Professionals in the Third Millennium', *The Electronic Library*, 26(2): 226–37.

15 There are many examples, such as the Radcliffe Science Library: http://www.bodleian.ox.ac.uk/science/use/3d-printing, accessed 25 August 2015.

16 Department of Business, Innovation and Skills (June 2011) *Higher Education: Students at the Heart of the System*, https://www.gov.uk/government/uploads/system/uploads/attachment_data/file/31384/11-944-higher-education-students-at-heart-of-system.pdf, accessed 10 September 2015.

17 Aestheticodes: http://aestheticodes.com/. Aestheticodes offer the interactivity of QR codes but in a more visually engaging experience.

18 T. Brabazon (2014) 'The Disintermediated Librarian and a Reintermediated Future', *The Australian Library Journal*, 63(3): 191–205.

19 S. Bains (2013) 'Teaching "Old" Librarians New Tricks', *SCONUL Focus*, 58.

20 B. Mathews (2014) 'Librarian as Futurist: Changing the Way Libraries Think About the Future', *Portal: Libraries and the Academy*, 14(3): 453–62.

21 A. R. Kenney (2015) 'From Engaging Liaison Librarians to Engaging Communities', *College & Research Libraries*, 76(3): 386–91.

22 K. J. Malenfant (2010) 'Leading Change in the System of Scholarly Communication: A Case Study of Engaging Liaison Librarians for Outreach to Faculty', *College and Research Libraries*, 71(1): 63–76.

23 M. Vandegrift and G. Colvin (2012) 'Relational Communications: Developing Key Connections', *College & Research Libraries News*, 73(7): 386–9.

24 A. M. Wright (2012) 'Starting Scholarly Conversations: A Scholarly Communication Outreach Program', *Journal of Librarianship and Scholarly Communication*, 2(1): 1–9.

25 P. C. Johnson (2014) 'International Open Access Week at Small to Medium U.S. Academic Libraries: The First Five Years', *The Journal of Academic Librarianship*, 40(6): 626–31.
26 Higher Education Funding Council for England (2015) *Open Access in the Next Research Excellence Framework: Policy Adjustments and Qualifications*, http://www.hefce.ac.uk/media/HEFCE,2014/Content/Pubs/2015/CL202015/Print-friendly%20version.pdf, accessed 25 August 2015.
27 The book *Oaths and Swearing in Ancient Greece* by Alan H. Sommerstein and Isabelle C. Torrance was published by De Gruyter. It is available through Knowledge Unlatched and The OAPEN Library.
28 S. Abram and J. Cromity (2013) 'Collaboration: The Strategic Core of 21 Century Library Strategies', *New Review of Information Networking*, 18(1): 40–50.
29 I. Silver (2014) 'Authors@UF Campus Conversation Series: A Case Study', *Public Services Quarterly*, 10(4): 263–82.
30 M. Posner (2013) 'No Half Measures: Overcoming Common Challenges to Doing Digital Humanities in the Library', *Journal of Library Administration*, 53: 43–52.

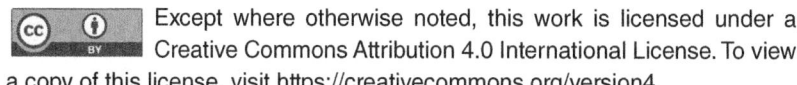 Except where otherwise noted, this work is licensed under a Creative Commons Attribution 4.0 International License. To view a copy of this license, visit https://creativecommons.org/version4

OPEN

9

Academic Libraries and Academic Books: Vessels of Cultural Continuity, Agents of Cultural Change

Kate Price

Abstract: *Academic books can deeply affect the ways that human beings perceive the world and interact with one another, playing an important role in cultural change. Academic libraries help to ensure that their contents are available to inform the thinking of future generations, playing an important role in cultural continuity.*

This chapter argues that the academic book may evolve into something very different in the future, but that the passion of librarians for ensuring that books in whatever form are made freely available will continue to drive forward innovation and collaboration, even in the face of major social and technological changes.

Keywords: culture; digital preservation; ebooks; ethics; librarianship

Lyons, Rebecca E. and Samantha J. Rayner (eds).
The Academic Book of the Future. Basingstoke: Palgrave Macmillan, 2016. DOI: 10.1057/9781137595775.0016.

This chapter examines the role that academic books play in culture beyond the academy, and the ways in which academic libraries and librarians can support and challenge that role as books move into the next stage of their evolution.

The *Oxford English Dictionary* defines culture as 'the distinctive ideas, customs, social behaviour, products, or way of life of a particular nation, society, people, or period'.[1] Whether an academic book appears as a traditionally published print-on-paper textbook, scholarly monograph or reference work, or as a more fluid digitally-produced work with interactive, collaborative or social media elements, it exists to encapsulate knowledge in some depth, and distribute it to all those who wish to learn from it, in the process becoming a powerful vector for the transmission of culture. However, the evolution of the academic book poses some major questions about the future role of both books and libraries in society.

Academic books as agents of cultural change

The fundamental quality of an academic book, in contrast to other forms of academic discourse such as the journal article or conference paper, is that it embodies a sustained and in-depth examination of a particular topic. Books are more suited to non-expert readership, as they allow the author space for full explanations which can move from the basic to the sophisticated within the course of a single work. This makes them particularly important as transmitters of new ideas within wider society as well as within the purely academic environment.

When an academic book is doing its job well, the author synthesises new and existing data and ideas into a cogent piece of work. The reader ingests these facts and concepts, and then a process of cognition takes place. The facts and concepts become transformed into wider knowledge, and a change occurs in the world as a consequence. The results may be quickly recognised at the individual level: the author may experience an increase in their academic reputation and gain a promotion; a student may be able to explain an idea that is new to them to a seminar group; a medical doctor may find the details of a new drug combination and use it to treat a patient; a member of the public may be inspired to pursue a topic further by visiting a historic site, and so on.

However, the effects of academic books can be much more profound, producing transformative changes at the cultural level. To give a very brief and partial selection of examples, Newton's *Principia Mathematica*, Darwin's *Origin of Species*, Marx's *Das Kapital*, Greer's *The Female Eunuch*, and Carson's *Silent Spring* profoundly changed our perception of the mechanics of the physical universe, the genesis of humanity, the effects of capitalist economics on society, the way that the sexes relate to one another, and the human effect on the environment.

It is important to remember that texts such as these have never stood alone. Each author was able to draw upon centuries of existing intellectual discourse in written form, whilst also being able to debate their ideas with contemporaries. Readers continued to add to the debate long after publication, in both academic and public forums. Each text has become a node in a network of knowledge extending backwards and forwards in time, and crossing social and geographical boundaries. Over time (and with the help of academic libraries which continued to make them available), such texts have weathered controversy and strong opposition to become the foundation stones for today's cultural attitudes.

In the digital world, academic texts are potentially more available to the public than ever before, with a corresponding potential for more immediate and wider effects on cultures and societies. It is now possible to publish and disseminate texts through a number of different channels, including Open Access formats that require no payment from the reader. It is also possible to access a book review or citation in one digital publication, or to be alerted to the existence of a book by a social media network, and then immediately download the full text of the work onto a mobile device, or order a print version online for delivery within a few hours. Online forums allow readers and authors to engage in debate surrounding the content, bringing it very swiftly to the attention of an expanding audience.

Although wider access to books is facilitated by digital advancements, it can also be restrictive. The cultural influence of the academic book is not lost on governments and political groups that seek to control the perceptions and behaviours of populations. The banning and deliberate destruction of books and purging of libraries has occurred in different cultural contexts throughout the ages, as a means of imposing religious or political orthodoxies. In the digital arena, where there are no physical copies to purge, governments are able to restrict access to digital book content simply by preventing public internet access altogether, as in

North Korea,[2] or by filtering internet content using blacklisted terms, as with the 'Great Firewall of China'.[3] Deliberate denial of access to academic books for political reasons is extreme, but there are many other challenges that lie in the way of public engagement with academic texts in the digital arena. Individual poverty, local or national lack of investment in digital infrastructure, lack of digital book content available in local languages, lack of user-friendliness in ebook interfaces, volatility of formats and business models, impermanence of content, lack of interlinking between digital texts, and differences in intellectual property rights law between nations all throw up practical barriers to accessing academic books in new media.

In the meantime, social factors such as lack of familiarity with the use of digital media amongst demographic groups such as the elderly,[4] a trend towards shallower engagement with online texts exemplified by the 'skimming' and 'bouncing' behaviours observed during the British Library's Information Behaviour of the Researcher of the Future project,[5] and a tendency towards accessing the online 'snippets' of visual and audio based content eloquently described by Nicholas Carr in his book *The Shallows*,[6] may lead to the inability of readers to make the most of the rich textual content to which they do have access.

Thus readers with less money, who live in poorly developed areas of the world, who are non-English speakers, who are less adept with online media, or who have less contact with long-form works in their previous experience are potentially even less likely to engage with academic books in the future than they are at present.

The issue of trust and quality also arises – readers may lack trust in content that does not bear a familiar brand, or conversely may be inclined to place too much trust in content that has been produced by pressure groups to reinforce the existing prejudices or exploit the vulnerabilities of their target audiences.

In the future, major challenges may also arise from the diversity and ephemerality of some of the discourse surrounding academic books. If it is important to be able to reconstruct the pathway of an argument by reading the original quotation in context, or correctly attribute the genesis of an idea, how might we access and cite these in the future when the content of social media is changing, and potentially disappearing, at an accelerating rate?

Academic libraries as vessels of cultural continuity

In common with academic books, academic libraries have encountered both huge opportunities and huge challenges as a consequence of the internet revolution and the social changes that this has brought about. Libraries (including national, university and college, learned society, and museum libraries) have played a critical role in the systematic collection and preservation of academic works for over two thousand years, and as such have been agents of cultural continuity, complementing the role that academic books play as agents of cultural change.

Academic libraries have also been pioneers, being amongst the first large organisations to harness the power of networked information dissemination, notably through the provision of online public access catalogues and online abstracting and indexing services such as IBSS (International Bibliography of the Social Sciences), which was produced by the British Library of Political and Economic Science at the London School of Economics between 1989 and 2010. However, over the last 20 years, the central role of libraries in the provision of academic information has been called into question by fast-developing internet services such Google, Wikipedia and Mendeley, which provide user-friendly conduits to academic texts without recourse to the library catalogue. These services, together with novel business models such as Open Access, have raised the possibility that the academic book of the future could be entirely de-coupled from the concept of the library collection. If this is the case, what are the implications for cultural continuity?

One of the defining characteristics of the academic library is that it curates a structured and quality-controlled collection of books suited to the needs of its specific audiences through cycles of selection, cataloguing and classification, physical or virtual arrangement, stock review, and relegation. In other words, curation is the process of deciding what to keep and how best to make it visible.

In the highly networked world of the academic book of the future, curation may appear to be irrelevant, as the physical location of a volume becomes unimportant and readers can find and use books directly from the authors' or publishers' websites. However, effective curation is hugely important when considering issues of cultural continuity, since born-digital information is at risk of loss almost as soon as it has been created, particularly if it includes social media elements, or if the technology upon which it is accessed becomes obsolete (consider, for instance, CD-ROMs). Also, the indiscriminate preservation of every single iteration of a fluid, digital text may render the core meaning of that text impossible to reconstruct at a later date.

To guarantee the long-term continuation of access to the fundamental message and meaning of the academic book of the future and its surrounding discourse, curatorial decisions need to be made on what elements should be retained at the time that the content is created, and arrangements need to be made for placing the content in a trusted repository. At present, there is no obvious way to do this systematically for all newly created digital works (particularly those which do not come to fruition via established publishing routes), to guarantee that this content will be discoverable in the future, or to ensure that such new works become situated in their academic and cultural context through backwards and forwards links.

Some publishers may place content into dark archiving services such as Portico and CLOCKSS to enable long-term preservation, as well as depositing the text with a national library. The Internet Archive and Hathi Trust also preserve digital books. The Directory of Open Access Books (DOAB) signposts peer-reviewed academic books published in Open Access formats, and thereby offers an element of quality control. CrossRef provides a clearing-house for links between works published online. Virtual distributed collections such as the European Library and the Digital Public Library of America (DPLA) showcase the outcomes of digitisation projects which may be preserved at individual institutions. OCLC's WorldCat service aims to provide a comprehensive global library catalogue. There is overlap or interplay between several of these services, which gives the sense of a patchwork of approaches to an evolving curatorial problem, without providing an overarching solution. However, the organisations that oversee and develop these services do provide possible models of governance, independent of individual author, institution or publisher interests, which could be built upon to provide systematic curatorial decision-making services for the future.

What is notable about the initiatives mentioned above is that although they do not bear the names of individual academic libraries, they have often been implemented as a result of issues highlighted by academic librarians, and continue to develop through the collaboration of librarians with other professional groups, across institutional and sectoral boundaries. The ethics and values of librarianship as a profession are instrumental in this approach. For example, the CILIP (Chartered

Institute of Library and Information Professionals) Ethical Principles emphasises 'concern for the public good... including respect for diversity within society, and the promoting of equal opportunities and human rights',[7] and as Professor Robert Darnton, up until recently Harvard's University Librarian, says of the DPLA, 'What could be more utopian than a project to make the cultural heritage of humanity available to all humans?'[8]

Such professional values have driven much of what has already been achieved in making academic books available online to ever wider audiences, and have moved some librarians to take strong positions on areas of concern ranging from Open Access and technical restrictions on the use of published text, to the provision of accessible versions of texts for disabled readers, many of which can be challenging for both authors and publishers. These professional values are the product of a particular culture (one of openness and inclusivity), and aim to continue it by providing a voice for current and future readers.

The emphasis on equitable access to information extends to the provision of facilities and support for the use of new forms of information. For example, King's College London makes available almost 200 laptop computers across six library sites to borrow free of charge to ensure that individuals are not disadvantaged if they cannot afford to purchase their own digital device,[9] and Manchester University Library's 'My Learning Essentials' programme[10] provides self-directed learning materials to assist students and researchers in assessing books' quality and relevance. In these and many other ways, libraries help readers to make full use of academic-book content, and thereby play a part in ensuring that the knowledge and understanding that books can provide continue to be part of our wider culture.

Conclusion

Academic books and academic libraries play important roles in the creation, transformation, and continuation of cultures and societies, informing the ways in which human beings perceive and interact with the world and one another. Although new means of communication, information provision and cultural expression may seriously challenge the position of books and libraries, it is likely that both will continue to evolve to meet those challenges.

Librarians will be essential partners with the authors and publishers of the academic book of the future during this process of evolution: by raising their awareness of issues of fundamental cultural importance, and by working with them to ensure that the network of knowledge linking the past to the present and onwards into the future remains intact to inform the thinking of future generations, librarians will continue to be custodians of our intellectual, cultural, and creative heritage. In summary, because of the passion of librarians for ensuring that books in whatever form are made freely available to everyone, along with the means to make good use of them, there is reason to believe that academic libraries will continue to be vessels of cultural continuity well into the future.

Notes

1 *Oxford English Dictionary* (2015) 'Culture, n.' in *OED Online* [database] (Oxford: Oxford University Press), accessed 22 August 2015.
2 M. Sparkes (23 December 2014) 'Internet in North Korea: Everything You Need to Know', *Daily Telegraph*, http://www.telegraph.co.uk/technology/11309882/Internet-in-North-Korea-everything-you-need-to-know.html, accessed 4 September 2015.
3 O. August (2007) 'The Great Firewall: China's Misguided – and Futile – Attempt to Control what Happens Online', *Wired Magazine*, 15(11), http://archive.wired.com/politics/security/magazine/15-11/ff_chinafirewall, accessed 4 September 2015.
4 For example, a recent study found that '44% of Americans aged 65 and older do not use the internet, and these older Americans make up almost half (49%) of non-internet users overall'. K. Zichuhr (2013), *Who's Not Online and Why* (Washington, DC: Pew Research Center), http://www.pewinternet.org/2013/09/25/whos-not-online-and-why/, accessed 4 September 2014.
5 I. Rowlands, D. Nicholas, P. Williams, et al. (2008) 'The Google Generation: The Information Behaviour of the Researcher of the Future', *Aslib Proceedings*, 60(4): 290–310.
6 N. G. Carr (2010) *The Shallows: How the Internet Is Changing the Way We Read, Think and Remember* (London: Atlantic Books).
7 CILIP (2004) 'Ethical Principles', CILIP website, http://www.cilip.org.uk/cilip/about/ethics/ethical-principles, accessed 22 August 2015.
8 R. Darnton (2013) 'The National Digital Public Library Is Launched!' *The New York Review of Books*, http://www.nybooks.com/articles/archives/2013/apr/25/national-digital-public-library-launched/, accessed 22 August 2015.

9   Library Services, King's College London (2015) 'Laptop Loans for Students', http://www.kcl.ac.uk/library/using/loans/laptops.aspx, accessed 22 August 2015.
10 University of Manchester Library (2015) *My Learning Essentials,* http://www.library.manchester.ac.uk/services-and-support/students/support-for-your-studies/my-learning-essentials, accessed 4 September 2015.

Except where otherwise noted, this work is licensed under a Creative Commons Attribution 4.0 International License. To view a copy of this license, visit https://creativecommons.org/version4

Part IV
Booksellers

OPEN

10
Selling Words: An Economic History of Bookselling

Jaki Hawker

Abstract: *A summary of the fiscal relationship between text, readers, publishers, bookshops, and legislation, this chapter argues that it is the economics of the consumer market that will shape the academic book of the future. Suggesting that demand for text intersects across a global marketplace, this chapter predicts a future in which the distinctions between physical and digital text, and Open Access and commercial publication, are so blurred as to be indistinguishable. Case studies from past, current, and future fiscal strategy illuminate the economics of reading, publishing and bookselling online and on the high street, and are used to consider a future where a marketplace governed by personal choice rather than publisher provision will determine textual form.*

Keywords: accessibility; bookselling; choice; consumer; demand; digital text; ebook; economics; innovation; market; Open Access; physical book; publishing; reading

Lyons, Rebecca E. and Samantha J. Rayner (eds).
The Academic Book of the Future. Basingstoke: Palgrave Macmillan, 2016. DOI: 10.1057/9781137595775.0018.

I make my living from words. Language is the primary currency of communication, and although my fiscal relationship with text may be a little more direct than yours (even if I am not, unlike Dickens, paid by the word but rather by the book) we all have an undeniable personal investment in the commerce of trafficking text. It is this relationship between markets, customers, and equations of supply and demand that I'm going to discuss in this chapter.

Academic texts, and platforms for disseminating academic texts, have changed faster and more fundamentally than any other sector of the bookselling market. Academic texts today encompass printed paper books and online digital learning; Open Access journals and peer-reviewed blog posts; text that is fixed and text that is infinitely flexible. Some academic resources may not be delivered in words at all; text to speech transcripts; image; sound or video. Equally, the exchange of currency that makes academic publication possible has evolved in tandem with publication methods. Publication is as likely today to be financed at the source as part of a research proposal, by a host institution, or by the author, as it is to be funded by post-publication purchase.

Whatever the text and however it is funded and curated, for a bookseller the primary factor in determining the success or failure of any project is success in the market, whether that success is measured in sales or in read counts. Arguably, it is that market, the textual consumer, the reader – of commercial or Open Access text – and their economic demands that will shape the future of academic text.

Pressure to publish ('publish or perish') accompanies most academic careers.[1] With tenure linked to publication, writing and re-writing papers for journals has become an end in itself, and publication citations are a necessary footnote to any academic profile. Even commissioned text may be unfunded or unpaid. While the volume of articles and papers submitted for publication increases yearly, librarians, spending on average 70 per cent of their materials budget on journals (thus accounting for the vast majority of journal sales[2]), are under immense pressure to cut costs. Journal publishers were quick to move to digital copy, but library purchasing of digital text has revealed an uneven demand, with some articles in constant circulation and others never accessed.[3] In conversation, when discussing digital publishing with academic librarians, two issues dominated: journal bundling and double dipping – attempts by traditional publishers to maximise a marketplace where digital data has revealed consumer choice and user-directed purchasing has become the selection criteria for purchase. Journal sales to libraries have inevitably decreased. As a result, while the pressure to publish will not diminish, the economic capacity of traditional publishers to support academic publication in either digital or physical form will continue to erode.

Given this combination of bloated product, decreasing market, and continued pressure to publish, it's not surprising that Open Access publishing was pioneered in the journal marketplace. In 1996, 24 per cent of papers published were made available through online Open Access sources. In 2014, that figure, supported by European legislation and both government and industry funding, was 50 per cent.[4] Free access promotes scholarship (The Hague Declaration[5]), and it would be easy to assume that the online journal publishing marketplace supported by new publishing houses is infinite. But it is not. Just as traditional journal publishing requires a market to be sustainable, so too does online publishing. The metrics may be different, with income deriving from pre-publication payments and library subscriptions, where financial success is measured by clicks rather than direct sales, but it is still a marketplace, and one affected inevitably by the mechanisms of demand and supply. At this point in time, in a rapidly developing online market, editors are hungry for content and contributors. As the market matures, financial viability and investment accountability will become the measure of publication, and as learning moves further online, as more students and academics access single articles rather than full journals, authors will be judged not only by peer review but by the actions of readers across the globe. Demand will inevitably govern content, and it's possible to conceive of text being judged not by peer review, but by the swipe-and-like judgement of a dating site model. No clicks, no sales or return on expenditure, no publishing contract. In this challenging environment, I'd argue that a critical examination of the impetus to publish is long overdue.

Traditional book publishers have been posing the same questions – *why publish?* – for years. The answer is that, despite the availability of both legitimate Open Access text and torrent downloads, readers still buy books. And for booksellers, academic books, lengthy explorations of a particular theme or concept, intended to instruct and elucidate a reader or a student, however broad the definition of student, are the heart of our trade.

Every year, I contact academic teaching staff and discuss their undergraduate and postgraduate reading lists. I plan launches for local publications and delve into publisher catalogues. I've watched lecturers develop the ways in which they use text for teaching across subject areas and platforms, spoken to editors and developers, explored digital learning and social media, and discussed text with students. I've seen initiatives succeed and fail in a market that changes every year. In these days of immediate student feedback and rapid technological development, change is both increasingly easy to quantify, with sales figures and read counts freely available, and more difficult to predict. Feedback does not always predict consumer choices, and publisher innovation is not always the best fit for a reader.

Student feedback has suggested that students want easy-to-access text cheaper, and preferably free.[6] With universities in England and Wales funding undergraduate tuition via student fees, this feedback has fuelled a move to university-funded ebooks and Open Access textbooks and journals. Publishers have responded with dedicated learning platforms and interactive text. Yet at the same time, student usage has suggested a very different picture. John Kelly of Oxford University Press reports that in 2014 only 6 per cent of students provided with an ebook and physical book bundle accessed the ebook; 35 per cent of students provided with an ebook and additional digital resources accessed both.[7] Ironically, that 35 per cent is exactly the proportion of students I would have expected to purchase a physical textbook if no digital text was provided. Even in courses where use of digital material is mandatory, 4 per cent of students never view those resources. Here in Edinburgh, two major courses moved to Open Access text following student feedback. Yet in 2013 and 2014, 25 per cent of those same students willingly purchased physical copies of a textbook they could read and use, free to them, online.[8]

The last ten years have seen many traditional publishers and start-ups develop new models of financing, structuring and using text. In the American market, where textbook prices leverage far higher publisher returns and corresponding student costs than in the UK (see Kirtsaeng v. John Wiley & Sons, Inc.[9]), just as in journal publishing, financial constraints have led to a corresponding rise in the Open Access text market. At first glance, Open Access offers a perfect solution to students. Text is freely available to both lecturer and student, fully accessible within the limitations of the platform chosen, and exclusive of copyright restraints. And yet. 'I don't like the text,' one lecturer confided to me. 'My students want free material, but this isn't the level I want to be teaching.' Open Access publisher Flat World lasted five years on start-up capital of $26.5 million before introducing charges for student access to text in 2012. It was already charging for lecturer access.[10] Bookboon, using material gathered from non-copyrighted text across the web to compile textbooks, kindly promises 'less than 15% advertising'.[11] I asked author and publisher David Diez of OpenIntro how he financed the print edition of his Open Access textbook. He laughed. 'Lots of volunteer labour,' he said. And I've raised a sardonic eyebrow at some Open Access textbooks priced, in their print versions, at well over the market rate for traditional textbooks. Don't forget the 25 per cent of students, educated through digital learning platforms throughout their school careers, who still use printed text, or the 80 per cent of teenagers purchasing print books in preference to ebooks.[12]

Studying the market for textbooks, in my experience the most successful innovations of the last five years have been paper and ebook bundles, where the same text is available in different formats but in a single purchase, and course-specific custom publications. Sales of these publications can outstrip traditional books by factors of up to 200 per cent. Paper and ebook bundles offer students choice, flexibility, portability and a competitive price, particularly useful for those universities folding textbook provision into student tuition fees. Custom textbooks are equally useful for a lecturer, offering dedicated text, although are far less popular with students tied to a unique purchase point. Both options may or may not come with dedicated course resources, although the relevance of those resources to the course being taught may vary.[13]

One innovation I've seen gaining ground this year is the custom textbook produced, not by the publisher or the lecturer, but as a collaborative enterprise involving both teaching staff and students on a particular course. These curated texts can be both physically and digitally available, tend to involve both interactive media and fixed text, and have often been constructed to respond rapidly to new research and findings in that particular study area.

The factors common to all these success stories is that they are mixed media creations, available on at least two platforms, containing text that includes a high degree of personalised content. They are structured towards active rather than passive reading, with students interacting with both text and lecturer through learning platforms, social media, and in class. Obviously, these are factors that do not necessarily translate to every academic book, but I do expect to see innovations undertaken for the lucrative student market spread to general academic publishing.

For me, the bottom line in considering the academic book of the future is not 'What does it look like?' but 'Does it sell?' If you'd asked me five years ago, I would not have predicted that in 2015 I'd still be working in an academic bookshop whose primary source of income remains physical textbook sales, supplemented but not replaced by digital sales. Now, I'm beginning to wonder if in 2020, students and academics will still prefer paper to pixels. It may look as though I'm arguing for the traditional print book, but what I'm actually saying is that it's very easy to be seduced by the bright lights of technological innovation without considering what readers want. And what readers want is choice, both in learning material, and in format.

Today, I expect academic publishers to print a revised edition of an out-of-date textbook in both digital and physical forms, provide online teaching resources for an iconic edition accessible across multiple devices, or commission a new manuscript about a particular area of study if the proposed title offers a new and credible interpretation. I expect publishers to offer a text that embraces new research and offers flexible update options online and in print. I expect searchable text, the capacity to store my library on a device no larger than the palm of my hand, and to be able to read in the bath. I expect to be running my fingers along my bookshelves and remember the places and times where I bought much loved editions of much loved books. I expect to engage with text, author, and publisher via social media and in person in my own bookshop. I also expect other readers to want different things from their own texts, and as a bookseller I want the capacity to be able to provide that choice.

I've talked at length about a market driven and financed by consumer demand, and of the ways in which I believe that the market – the reader's choices and preferences – will shape the academic text of the future. But there are other aspects to a global marketplace and consumer culture, with little financial muscle but of immense social influence, which I trust and hope will enhance academic text in the future. The ability to access the printed word is not available to every consumer. Text to speech, variable on-screen text justification, accessible texts, fonts and backgrounds, visual rather than textual explanation, animation rather than tabular data description are all innovations deriving from a marketplace which is not yet financially powerful, but will be. As learning becomes a truly international activity, the demand for accessible text will grow, and resources devoted to development and publication will be correspondingly greater. Of all the options the creators of academic text will explore in the future,

DOI: 10.1057/9781137595775.0018

of all the excitement creative choice will bring to reading, this particular option is my own personal favourite textual future. I'd argue that the book of the future will be inclusive, collaborative, available across multiple platforms and in a number of formats. Whether pre- or post-publication funded, I'd also expect that book to be financially viable. Bookshops, successful bookshops, online or in a university, make hard choices. If a book doesn't sell, and if there is no market, you're not going to find it on our shelves. It's very easy to predict, in the excitement and discovery of Open Access text and learning platform development, with print on demand capacity and custom publications, that the future of text contains infinite possibilities. Perhaps it does. But I believe, just as a bookshop makes choices governed by the consumers, those infinite possibilities will be created, enabled and shaped, by the market. In my eyes, it is our readers and their personal and financial choices who are as important in the creation of text as the publisher, and it is the reader who will determine the success or failure of any textual project, whatever form that project may take.

Luckily, we're all readers.

Notes

1. C. Cerejo (2013) 'Navigating through the Pressure to Publish', *Editage Insights*, http://www.editage.com/insights/navigating-through-the-pressure-to-publish/, accessed 4 September 2015.
2. Publishers Communications Group (2015) *Library Budget Predictions for 2015*, http://www.pcgplus.com/wp-content/uploads/2015/01/Library-Budget-Predictions-for-2015.pdf, accessed 7 August 2015.
3. É. Archambault, D. Amyot, P. Deschamps, A. Nicol, F. Provencher, L. Rebout and G. Roberge (2014) *Proportion of Open Access Papers Published in Peer-Reviewed Journals at the European and World Levels 1996–2013*, http://science-metrix.com/files/science-metrix/publications/d_1.8_sm_ec_dg-rtd_proportion_oa_1996-2013_v11p.pdf, accessed 7 August 2015.
4. J. Priem, D. Taraborelli, P. Groth and C. Neylon (2010) *Altmetrics: A Manifesto*, http://altmetrics.org/manifesto, accessed 4 September 2015.
5. LIBER (2015) *The Hague Declaration on Knowledge Discovery in the Digital Age*, http://thehaguedeclaration.com, accessed 7 August 2015
6. Student feedback panels, The Academic Professional and Specialist Group Conference (Booksellers Association) 2013, 2014, 2015. Most recent programme, www.booksellers.org.uk, accessed 10 July 2015

7   J. Kelly (May 2015). Internal company reporting in conversation with Jaki Hawker.
8   J. Hawker. Internal company sales reports, Blackwell's.
9   Supreme Court Kirtsaeng v. John Wiley & Sons, Inc., http://www.supremecourt.gov (home page), accessed 7 August 2015.
10 D. Lederman (2012) 'Fleeing rom "Free"', *Inside Higher Ed*, https://www.insidehighered.com/news/2012/11/05/flat-worlds-shift-gears-and-what-it-means-open-textbook-publishing, accessed 7 August 2015.
11 Bookboon blog (600+ Open Access textbooks), http://bookboon.com, accessed 7 August 2015.
12 E. Drabble (16 December 2014) 'Teens Prefer the Printed Page to ebooks', *Guardian*, http://www.theguardian.com/childrens-books-site/2014/dec/16/teens-ebooks-ereaders-survey, accessed 7 August 2015.
13 I. Lapowsky (2015) 'What Schools Must Learn from LA's iPad Debacle', *Wired*, http://www.wired.com/2015/05/los-angeles-edtech/, accessed 7 August 2015.

Except where otherwise noted, this work is licensed under a Creative Commons Attribution 4.0 International License. To view a copy of this license, visit https://creativecommons.org/version4

OPEN

11

The Future of the Academic Book: The Role of Booksellers

Peter Lake

Abstract: *Universities, lecturers, and students are faced with a plethora of choice when it comes to courseware, choices that both complement and replace the traditional textbook. The future role of university booksellers will be to provide the best discovery, delivery, and evaluation tools to help lecturers and students choose and get the most benefit from their learning resources. Whilst booksellers will continue to offer a retail presence for students, their business model will evolve and become more reliant on services and software revenues from universities.*

Keywords: booksellers; courseware; delivery; discovery; evaluation; learning resources; services; software; textbook

Lyons, Rebecca E. and Samantha J. Rayner (eds). *The Academic Book of the Future.* Basingstoke: Palgrave Macmillan, 2016. DOI: 10.1057/9781137595775.0019.

At a time when the global demand for tertiary education is at its highest and set for sustained growth in the years to come, textbooks, so long a staple of undergraduate courses, are in decline. Student numbers are going up, sales of textbooks in all formats are going down and their traditional role as the supporting guide or narrative to a subject is being challenged. Growth in demand for tertiary education and the impact of the Internet and the networked society on how that education is delivered mean that students and educators now have a much wider and richer array of learning resources (referred to here as 'courseware' for convenience) to support course delivery, study and student success. This chapter focusses on the undergraduate textbook as this has long been the main product offered by university booksellers. What is the future role for those booksellers as universities and students adopt new ways of course delivery and new courseware?

That textbooks are in decline is not a surprise. The networked society has not been kind to the traditional content providers. The music, film, newspaper, and publishing industries have all been disrupted as consumers become producers and make their music available via file-sharing services and their videos on YouTube whilst disseminating knowledge on Wikipedia and obtaining and spreading news on social media. Many established players have faltered, new digital competition has emerged, and publishers are rethinking their business models and value propositions.

Perhaps the surprise is how well textbooks continue to perform compared to other areas of publishing such as business, professional, and financial, where online and data-driven solutions have all but replaced the book. In part this is due to the fact that textbooks do their job well – providing a well-structured and user-friendly guide to a topic and, in part, due to the naturally cautious approach of faculty to making changes to the way established modules and courses are delivered.

But this is changing as some major trends impact on how universities deliver their courses. First, the increase in demand for tertiary education is challenging the traditional university model. Globally, the tertiary education participation rate for 25–34-year-olds has increased to just shy of 40 per cent compared with 25 per cent for 55–64-year-olds with most of this growth coming from Asia and emerging markets. The traditional university model, despite new universities being established, cannot meet this demand, and there is a strong growth in distance learning, with new digital platforms being deployed to meet this demand.

Allied to this has been the growth in massive open online courses (MOOCs), some carrying college credits. Over 6 million students are enrolled on MOOCS, some of which are taught by among the most distinguished of professors. MOOCs have not only been part of the response to the increasing demand for tertiary education but have also been a clear demonstration of the potential for lecture capture, live streaming and video-on-demand as a core component of course delivery. A second trend is the flipped classroom and blended learning where instructional content is delivered outside the lecture hall, with lectures becoming smaller, discussion-based groups. Students do their research outside of lectures by watching online lectures, collaborating in online discussions and, of course, accessing and reading recommended books. Textbooks from commercial publishers still play a part, but they are now joined by open textbooks, MOOCs, online lectures and other resources, including lecturer-authored material. Add to this mix student vloggers, the impact of gaming on how content is presented and experienced and the rise of automated paper production based on text mining, and it is clear that courseware now comes in multiple formats, from multiple suppliers with competing business models.

Another reason the textbook may be less relevant in the future: publishers are racing to replace them with new digital services. These new services blend traditional textbook content with adaptive learning technologies, embedded testing and assessment features, integrated assignment functionality, personal study wallets and records, and collaborative learning tools. These services are being widely adopted in the US and there are some very encouraging indications that these more personalised learning pathways are producing better results for students and educators.

So if the university bookseller is going to be selling fewer textbooks, what will its role be in the future? Traditionally, the bookseller has been on campus providing a retail service to students and working with faculty on the selection and sourcing of the most appropriate learning resources. That business model will have to change and evolve. The student retail model will certainly persist and change as a broader range of goods and services will be offered to students. The move to digital and new forms of courseware will, however, make on-campus retailing uneconomic at some universities. Overall, the emphasis for booksellers will shift to providing services, software and solutions to universities. It already has in a number of markets.

There will be three main components of this shift: investment in and development of learning resources management services; digital content delivery platforms; and data analytic services. Behind the development of all three is the knowledge that with the wide range of courseware now available to universities only a very small percentage of their requirements are ever going to be met by a single supplier or single service. Lecturers and universities will be taking resources from multiple sources and booksellers are well placed to work with universities on the selection of resources, their deployment and integration, and in providing evaluation tools.

Learning resource management will be a key enabler for universities going forward as they blend resources from multiple providers and in multiple formats with their own self-generated resources. Booksellers are already helping with the discovery and selection of resources, with services such as Barnes & Noble College's Faculty Enlight, Amazon's CourseMaterials Tool, and Follett's Faculty Discover. Although these services have a focus on textbooks, they are already broadening their coverage to include MOOCs, open educational resources, YouTube videos, and have facilities for lecturers to upload and include their own material. Soon, all courseware will be covered and as part of the discovery process lecturers will be able to see what is being used at other institutions and to share their recommendations and experiences. As well as discovery and selection, these services will offer value for money assessment and purchasing options to help with budgeting and planning. And, of course, these services will not only be valuable to lecturers but will also be used by students. There will quickly develop a comprehensive database of student opinion and feedback that will inform both courseware selection and the future value proposition development of publishers and others.

Digital content platforms are another area of development for booksellers, with services such as Yuzu, Blackwells Learning and Kortext. Today these are ebook platforms that offer the benefit of aggregation and integration. Universities want ebooks tightly integrated with their virtual learning environments (VLEs) so it makes sense to specify only one platform for any given institution to deliver content from multiple suppliers. The focus for most of these ebook platforms, therefore, is not on selling directly to students but rather working with universities to provide students with a common ebook experience and to work with lecturers in integrating specific pieces of content into their VLE module design. This also fits in with the trend in some markets for courseware to be provided to students by their university as part of their course fee.

A second, important market for these platforms is and will be governments in a number of emerging markets where ebooks offer a more reliable route of getting textbooks to students, especially the high percentage of distance learners in these markets. As these platforms develop, they will offer the benefit of disaggregation as content provision will move to open-market models, and content owners will allow much more customer-defined purchasing of packages of content to be used within lecturer-curated courseware. With this in mind, the capabilities of these platforms are being expanded to include integration with adaptive learning software and will offer lecturers both authoring tools and course-building functionality. Finally, these platforms will offer all the multiple types of courseware available to lecturers and students locally and will provide seamless integration into any and all of the publishers' new services that are centrally hosted.

The third area of development is in analytics and evaluation services. The economic benefits of tertiary education remain very compelling: across the Organisation for Economic Co-operation and Development (OECD) the lifetime earning capacity for someone with a tertiary education is 50 per cent greater than someone with a higher secondary one.[1] The cost of providing that education is also increasing, either as a cost to the general taxpayer, or in the fees charged to or debts accumulated by students. Governments, universities, and students all have a significant interest in the most effective learning pathways and in developing employability skills alongside academic skills. Reducing the time and cost to gain a degree and/or increasing the social and economic benefit of a degree are key policy areas.

Booksellers are already working with universities on providing data and analysis that, for example, compares the impact of lecture attendance, library usage, and textbook usage to degree outcomes (attendance and textbook usage are highly correlated to degree outcomes, library usage less so). They are working with lecturers on analysing different patterns of ebook usage within student cohorts and feeding data into student engagement systems. This is really just the tip of an iceberg as more and more data will be available to universities on how, where, and when students study.

Data models will be developed to include all courseware usage, VLE usage, library and library platform usage, attendance, and work completion data alongside levels of interaction with fellow students and lecturers. In some instances, booksellers will help develop these models and services – especially those who work with a number of universities within a market – whilst in many others they will be able to provide university specific and comparative data on the effectiveness of the different courseware available to institutions. Booksellers will work with universities and lecturers on determining what is the best combination of content, tools, and platforms for producing the best outcomes for their students.

So from one perspective the primary role of booksellers will not change: in the future booksellers will still provide a retail service to students and will still work with faculty on the selection and sourcing of the most appropriate learning resources. But the bookselling business model will change. The retail offer will remain, and will have to broaden to remain economically viable. However, the investment and development focus, particularly for the larger booksellers will shift and will be on developing richer resources, platforms, and data to help universities provide the best courseware and learning outcomes for their students. In doing this, booksellers will focus more on their core asset: a deep understanding of and relationship with universities, lecturers, and students. As a result, they will find new, exciting ways to support university and student success.

Note

1 See OECD (2014) *Education at a Glance 2014: OECD Indicators*, http://www.oecd.org/edu/Education-at-a-Glance-2014.pdf, accessed 9 September 2015.

Except where otherwise noted, this work is licensed under a Creative Commons Attribution 4.0 International License. To view a copy of this license, visit https://creativecommons.org/version4

OPEN

12

Back to the Future: The Role of the Campus Bookshop

Craig Dadds

Abstract: *Campus booksellers with close links to their university play an essential role in supporting the academic activity of students and the research work of staff, as well as the cultural life of the university. This assertion was overwhelmingly supported by feedback from one hundred members of the academic community at Canterbury Christ Church University during a Periodic Departmental Review of Library Services in November 2014. When there is so much emphasis on providing the ultimate student experience – an academic bookshop on campus is a key asset.*

Keywords: academic; bookseller; bookselling; bookshop; campus; Canterbury Christ Church University; collaboration; learning community; partnership; student; student experience; university; university owned

Lyons, Rebecca E. and Samantha J. Rayner (eds).
The Academic Book of the Future. Basingstoke: Palgrave Macmillan, 2016. DOI: 10.1057/9781137595775.0020.

Whatever format the academic book of the future predominantly takes – whether virtual or physical – it is about providing options for our students and academics. In the book trade the only thing certain since the demise of the Net Book Agreement in 1995 is that we must expect the unexpected, and roll with the times. But we need to do more than roll with the times – we need to take charge and create opportunities. And we will do this by working together with not just publishers and librarians – but with our lecturers, as colleagues and authors, and with our students and customers.

As curators of content, our academic libraries and bookshops continue to play an undeniably important role in the experience of what it means to be educated and entertained. Bookshops and libraries are not merely noodle factories as acknowledged by Kurt Vonnegut in his wonderful speech of 1976 dedicating the new library at Connecticut College, New London.[1] They are worked by experienced and dedicated crews of librarians and booksellers. And – to paraphrase Neil Gaiman – unlike a Google search, which will return you 100,000 answers, these navigators of knowledge are able to bring you back the right one. In the New World of online marvels, we must not lose sight of the physical artefact, which will continue to play an important role. The book has always been about collaboration, in its production and dissemination, in its journey from author to reader – it is ideas made flesh. In this sense its ebook offspring should be no different.

Books can be purchased and accessed in hard copy and by online retrieval. In the future, academic bookshops will survive as clicks and mortar, adopting online purchasing and smartcard technology; by emphasising the tactile experience of browsing; by expanding product range and services; by offering author signings; workshops and events. So it is not an either/or question of ebook or hard copy; escalators or stairs; or whether these storehouses become impersonal keyboards and clicks, or shelves lined with beautifully produced books. They must provide for both: the existence of bookshops serving their communities – university or high street – is vital to our cultural well-being. That is at the heart of the matter. We must ensure bookshops do not become redundant in the delivery of content – whatever form that content takes.

> We estimate that when a bookshop closes, about a third of its sales transfer to another bookshop. This means as much as two thirds of sales disappear. Some of this spend doubtless migrates online; but much of it vanishes from the book sector entirely.[2]

A Periodic Departmental Review of Library Services took place at Canterbury Christ Church University (CCCU) in November 2014. What follows is a summary of the overwhelmingly positive response from one hundred CCCU academics when asked by email: What are the benefits of an academic bookshop on campus?[3]

The benefits of a bookshop seem too obvious to annunciate – to quote an anonymous bookseller: 'Words cannot do justice to the pleasures of a good bookshop. Ironically.' In testimonials received from CCCU academic staff an outpouring of support emerged, not only regarding the value of a physical bookshop on campus, but in particular one that is university-owned. A Booker Prize shortlisted author, the Programme Director for our MA in Creative Writing, commented:

> In my four years at CCCU, the one thing that has truly impressed me, and that is a match for any institution in the world, is the campus bookshop.

Another respondent said the university bookshop is a 'centre of text at the heart of campus' and 'a symbol of academic rigour and learning'. It demonstrates in a very physical manner what is involved in the work of a university. The bookshop promotes this not only to current undergraduates, researchers, and conference delegates throughout the year; but to prospective students on open days, to guest speakers and external examiners, and to visiting overseas academics from partner institutions. The bookshop, with its in-store and window displays, is 'one of the few places [on campus] where there are obvious clues of academic life', according to another responder.

The bookshop contributes to academic life by the promotion and provision of resources. A core activity, delivered in close partnership with academic staff, is the collation and production of recommended title reading lists which, one responder highlighted, 'enable students to turn up to classes with books, prepared and ready to participate'. The curation of recommended books relevant to subject areas studied at CCCU is vital. As is the speedy replenishment of stock on a 'just-in-time' basis, and customer orders that are ready for collection the following day, all with an automatic discount. It isn't just about selling books, it is about meeting customer needs and providing our students with options when it comes to accessing information and acquiring knowledge; whether that is an ebook, a second-hand purchase or borrowing a title from the university library. Booksellers are happy to price-check against online sellers because, contrary to popular belief, it is not always cheaper online.

By working closely with publishers and academic staff, the availability of custom books and 'book bundles' ensure good value. Our bookshop benefits immensely from its inclusion within the Department of Library Services at CCCU. Our staff regularly help students search the library database. Libraries do not put bookshops out of business. Where texts are too expensive, they can be borrowed or accessed; but ebook users continue to use bookshops.

Approachable and knowledgeable booksellers are crucial. It is necessary to pass the 'good bookshop test' – is being able to 'find books when you are not looking for anything in particular' or books the browser 'wouldn't have found on their own'. This 'browsability' was more recently termed by Mark Forsyth as 'the unknown unknown', in a specially commissioned Books Are My Bag promotional title.[4] The online bookseller equivalent is their 'also bought' selections. The bookshop offers a valuable physical space when it comes to taking time out from the pressures and demands of everyday academic life; it is 'a place for staff and students to wander among ideas and to generate chance sparks of inspiration'. The university bookshop is an 'essential part of the student experience at CCCU' but also 'supports the teaching and research of staff magnificently' as illustrated in the following anecdotes:

> Recently, I tried to buy an obscure, almost out of print book on Elizabeth I from a) Amazon and b) the Publisher to no avail (they only had three copies and couldn't find them). The CCCU bookshop was the only outlet that found me a copy, I rest my case.
>
> I know that I can ask for a book that the library do not stock and you can find it and have it 'in House' within days. This makes my work more research focused, more up to date and more effective. It is something I particularly value, even if I am not sure of the title and only know I need a book by Husserl!!
>
> Only this morning I was approached after class by an anxious international student who needed some reading guidance and wanted titles recommended to her. I was able to walk her into the bookshop and put the appropriate volumes straight into her hand. Problem solved.

Other academics have argued that the presence of a university-owned bookshop on campus 'adds to our image as a Place of Learning'. It is an 'essential part of a learning community'; and a 'powerful message of intent and delivery, of what, as a university, we are all about'. It has been described as 'CCCU at its best', and its booksellers as 'book ambassadors who go into the world holding a CCCU banner'. Like many high-street bookshops, the university bookshop is a modern, welcoming retail environment with seating and an adjacent Touchdown Café; but as a university-owned bookshop:

> It underscores the open-ended quest for understanding and enlightenment that must surely be at the heart of a Church-founded institution of Higher Education ... without it we're in danger of reducing education to the level of a purely financial transaction.
>
> It belongs to us – we can have a say in what is provided, stocked and offered to staff and students in a timely way. It is run by colleagues who understand our programmes, our requirements, and who are open to new ways of working. They are student and staff centric, they go the extra mile.

The university bookshop helps students identify with the university; and like the library, chapel, sports centre, art gallery, and student union it is an essential part of the student experience. The bookshop's Twitter account (@cccubookshop) has received many positive direct messages and tweets from followers external to CCCU lamenting the absence of a bookshop at their university.

During open days introductory texts are recommended to those interested in courses at CCCU, and such engagement might make all the difference in terms of converting prospective students to new students. Including the open days, bookselling at CCCU has evolved 'to meet the disparate needs of different campuses and respond to the diverse mix of programmes'.

Ownership allows for a closer working partnership with CCCU academic staff across all faculties and schools; as well as with colleagues in the library, and many other professional service departments. The bookshop stock is organised to reflect the faculty/school structure at CCCU. One section is dedicated to publications authored by CCCU academic staff; as well as CCCU students. This demonstrates to our students (and the general public) how tutors are actively engaged in research, exemplifying scholarship in their field of expertise. Publications by students are also promoted and displayed:

> The shop promotes local and/or lesser known visiting writers and smaller presses in a way that the large chains will simply not do.

The bookshop distributes CCCU publications such as John Lea's *77 Things to Think About: Teaching and Learning in Higher Education* (2012). Currently discussions are under way to investigate the potential of creating a CCCU Press, making postgraduate work readily available online and in a printed format.

The bookshop supports the university's public lecture series, as well as conferences and author signings. The latter is sponsored by the School of Humanities, and the Faculty of Education at CCCU. Authors recently included Esther Freud and Louis de Bernières with forthcoming readings from John Boyne, Michael Morpurgo, and Shami Chakrabarti planned for 2015–16. In total 34 events were organised by the bookshop in the last academic year. These are a form of outreach opening the university to the local community and supporting the university's widening participation agenda. As one respondent stated, the university is 'actively recruiting many students who have grown up in homes with no books' and 'some of whom live in areas with no bookshops, or small bookshops with only a very limited range of bestselling titles'. Conferences and book signings, with Michael Rosen or Anthony Browne, have resulted in more books in school classrooms and in the hands of teachers and pupils. Attending university is an exciting but potentially daunting prospect and according to one academic 'the presence of an in-house bookshop and a friendly face ... could mean the difference between a student being a proud graduate or not'.

> If our mission is to develop knowledge and pedagogic practice for our students and the community at large, the bookshop is in the forefront of supporting this essential role.

Notes

1 K. Vonnegut (1994) *Welcome to the Monkey House, Palm Sunday: An Autobiographical Collage* (London: Vintage Books), pp. 469–77.
2 D. McCabe (2013) 'Why Bookshops Matter', *The Bookseller*, http://www.thebookseller.com/blogs/why-bookshops-matter, accessed 4 September 2015.
3 Responses from CCCU staff have been anonymised.
4 M. Forsyth (2014) *Bookshops and the Delight of Not Getting What You Wanted* (London: Icon Books).

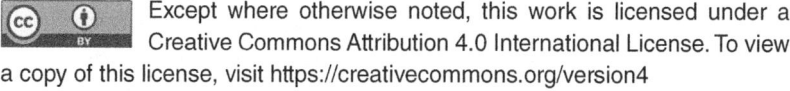 Except where otherwise noted, this work is licensed under a Creative Commons Attribution 4.0 International License. To view a copy of this license, visit https://creativecommons.org/version4

Bibliography

AAUP (2014) 'Library–Press Connections at the Charleston Conference', *AAUP website*, http://www.aaupnet.org/news-a-publications/aaup-publications/the-exchange/current-issue/1265-charleston-2014, accessed 20 August 2015.

AAUP website, http://www.aaupnet.org/index.php, accessed 20 August 2015.

Abba, T. (2013) 'The Future of the Book Shouldn't Be Skeuomorphic', *New Statesman*, http://www.newstatesman.com/culture/2013/02/future-book-shouldnt-be-skeuomorphic, accessed 25 August 2015.

Abbot, A. (27 June 2008) 'Publication and the Future of Knowledge', *Presentation to the Association of American University Presses*, http://home.uchicago.edu/~aabbott/Papers/aaup.pdf, accessed 20 August 2015.

Abram, S. and J. Cromity (2013) 'Collaboration: The Strategic Core of 21 Century Library Strategies', *New Review of Information Networking*, 18(1): 40–50.

Aestheticodes (2015) http://aestheticodes.com/, accessed 10 September 2015

Andersen, B. and S. Larsen (2012) 'Being a National Library in a Research Infrastructure Landscape', *Microfilm and Digitization Review*, 41(3–4): 175–79.

Archambault, É., D. Amyot, P. Deschamps, A. Nicol, F. Provencher, L. Rebout and G. Roberge (2014) *Proportion of Open Access Papers Published in Peer-Reviewed Journals at the European and World Levels 1996–2013*, http://science-metrix.com/files/science-metrix/publications/d_1.8_sm_ec_dg-rtd_proportion_oa_1996-2013_v11p.pdf, accessed 7 August 2015.

August, O. (2007) 'The Great Firewall: China's Misguided – and Futile – Attempt to Control What Happens Online', *Wired*, 15(11), http://archive.wired.com/politics/security/magazine/15-11/ff_chinafirewall, accessed 4 September 2015.

Ayris, P., E. McLaren, M. Moyle, C. Sharp and L. Speicher (2014) 'Open Access in UCL: A New Paradigm for London's Global University in Research Support', *Australian Academic & Research Libraries*, 45(4): 282–95.

Bains, S. (2013) 'Teaching "Old" Librarians New Tricks', *SCONUL Focus*, 58.

Ball, C. (7 October 2014) 'Proposal to The Andrew W. Mellon Foundation', in Dr Cheryl E. Ball (ed.) *An Academic Portfolio*, http://ceball.com/wp-content/uploads/2015/01/PORTFOLIO-COPY-WEB.pdf, accessed 20 August 2015.

Baron, N. (2015) *Words Onscreen: The Fate of Reading in a Digital World* (Oxford: Oxford University Press).

Barrett, E. and B. Bolt (eds) (2007) *Practice as Research: Approaches to Creative Arts Enquiry* (London: I.B. Tauris).

Bookboon, http://bookboon.com, accessed 7 August 2015.

Booksellers Association, www.booksellers.org.uk, accessed 10 July 2015

Borgman, C. (2015) *Big Data, Little Data, No Data* (Boston: MIT Press).

Brabazon, T. (2014) 'The Disintermediated Librarian and a Reintermediated Future', *The Australian Library Journal*, 63(3): 191–205.

Bresland, J. (2010) 'On the Origin of the Video Essay', *TriQuarterly*, 9(1), http://www.northwestern.edu/newscenter/stories/2013/07/the-video-essay-celebrating-an-exciting-new-literary-form.html#sthash.BpuwQbrG.dpuf, accessed 15 August 2015.

Burridge, S. (2013) '5 minutes with Sam Burridge: "Palgrave Pivot is Liberating Scholarship from the Straitjacket of Traditional Print-Based Formats and Business Models"', *LSE Review of Books*, http://blogs.lse.ac.uk/lsereviewofbooks/2013/10/28/palgrave-pivot-100-hours/, accessed 10 September 2015.

Campbell, C. (1990) 'The Future of Scholarly Communication', in K. Brookfield (ed.) *Scholarly Communication and Serials Prices: Proceedings of a Conference Sponsored by The Standing Conference of National and University Libraries and The British Library Research and Development Department*, 11–13 (London: Bowker-Saur).

Carr, N. (2011) *The Shallows: What the Internet is Doing to Our Brains* (New York: Norton).

Carr, N. G. (2010) *The Shallows: How the Internet is Changing the Way We Read, Think and Remember* (London: Atlantic Books).
Cassuto, L. (12 August 2013) 'The Rise of the Mini-Monograph', *The Chronicle of Higher Education*, http://chronicle.com/article/The-Rise-of-the-Mini-Monograph/141007/, accessed 20 August 2015.
Cathro, W. (2006) 'The Role of a National Library in Supporting Information Infrastructure', *Official Journal of the International Federation of Library Associations and Institutions*, 32(4): 333–39.
Cerejo, C. (2013) 'Navigating through the Pressure to Publish,' *Editage Insights*, http://www.editage.com/insights/navigating-through-the-pressure-to-publish, accessed 4 September 2015.
CILIP (2004) 'Ethical principles', *CILIP website*, http://www.cilip.org.uk/cilip/about/ethics/ethical-principles, accessed 22 August 2015.
Coelho, C. (12 January 2015) 'Mellon Grant to Fund Digital Scholarship Initiative', *Brown University website*, https://news.brown.edu/articles/2015/01/digital, accessed 20 August 2015.
Collins E. and G. Stone (2014) 'Open Access Monographs and the Role of the Library', *Insights – OA Monograph Supplement*, 11–16.
Cond, A. (18 August 2015) 'The University Press Is Back in Vogue', *The Bookseller* (blog), http://www.thebookseller.com/blogs/anthony-cond-309360, accessed 20 August 2015.
Costanzo, P. (23 May 2014) 'The Real Reason Enhanced Ebooks Haven't Taken Off (Or, Evan Schnittman Was Right … for the Most Part)', *Digital Book World*, http://www.digitalbookworld.com/2014/the-real-reason-enhanced-ebooks-havent-taken-off-or-evan-schnittman-was-right-for-the-most-part/, accessed 15 August 2015.
Crossick, G. (2014) *Monographs and Open Access: A Report to HEFCE*, http://www.hefce.ac.uk/media/hefce/content/pubs/indirreports/2015/Monographs,and,open,access/2014_monographs.pdf, accessed 20 August 2015.
Darnton, R. (2013) 'The National Digital Public Library Is Launched!' *The New York Review of Books*, http://www.nybooks.com/articles/archives/2013/apr/25/national-digital-public-library-launched, accessed 22 August 2015.
Deegan, M. and K. Sutherland (2009) *Transferred Illusions: Digital Technology and the Forms of Print* (London: Ashgate).
Department of Business, Innovation and Skills (June 2011) *Higher Education: Students at the Heart of the System*, https://www.gov.uk/government/uploads/system/uploads/attachment_data/

file/31384/11-944-higher-education-students-at-heart-of-system.pdf, accessed 10 September 2015.

Dickinson, T. (2015) 'Free core e-textbooks: a practical way to support students', http://www.cilip.org.uk/cilip/blog/free-core-e-textbooks-practical-way-support-students, accessed 25 August 2015.

Drabble, E. (16 December 2014) 'Teens Prefer the Printed Page to ebooks', *Guardian*, http://www.theguardian.com/childrens-books-site/2014/dec/16/teens-ebooks-ereaders-survey, accessed 7 August 2015.

Ebook Architects website, http://ebookarchitects.com/learn-about-ebooks/enhanced-ebooks/, accessed 15 August 2015.

Eisenstein, E. (1980) *The Printing Press as an Agent of Change* (Cambridge: Cambridge University Press).

Esposito, J. (7 March 2011) 'The New Economics of the University Press – A Report from the AAUP', *Scholarly Kitchen* (blog), http://scholarlykitchen.sspnet.org/2011/03/07/the-new-economics-of-the-university-press-a-report-from-the-aaup/, accessed 20 August 2015.

Febvre, L. and Henri-Jean Martin (1976) *The Coming of the Book: The Impact of Printing, 1450–1850*, trans. D. Gerard (New York: Verso).

Fitzpatrick, K. (2011) *Planned Obsolescence: Publishing, Technology, and the Future of the Academy* (New York: New York University Press).

Forsyth, M. (2014) *Bookshops and the Delight of Not Getting What You Wanted* (London: Icon Books).

Grant, C. (2013) 'Déjà-Viewing? Videographic Experiments in Intertextual Film Studies', *Mediascape* (Winter), http://www.tft.ucla.edu/mediascape/Winter2013_DejaViewing.html, accessed 21 August.

Grant, C. *AUDIOVISUALCY: Videographic Film and Moving Image Studies*, https://vimeo.com/groups/audiovisualcy, accessed 10 September 2015.

Hagerlid, J. (2011) 'The Role of the National Library as a Catalyst for an Open Access Agenda: The Experience of Sweden', *Interlending and Document Supply*, 39(2): 115–18

HEFCE (2015) 'Expert Panels', *REF 2014*, http://www.ref.ac.uk/panels/, accessed 4 August 2015.

Higher Education Funding Council for England (2015) *Open Access in the Next Research Excellence Framework: Policy Adjustments and Qualifications*, http://www.hefce.ac.uk/media/HEFCE,2014/Content/Pubs/2015/CL202015/Print-friendly%20version.pdf, accessed 25 August 2015.

Howard, J. (24 June 2013) 'For University Presses, a Time of Fixing Bridges, and Building New Ones', *The Chronicle of Higher Education*, http://chronicle.com/article/For-University-Presses-a-Time/139983/, accessed 20 August 2015.

Jisc (2014) 'Institution as e-textbook Publisher', *Jisc Collections website*, https://www.jisc-collections.ac.uk/Institution-as-E-textbook-Publisher/, accessed 20 August 2015.

Johns, A. (2000) *The Nature of the Book: Print and Knowledge in the Making* (Chicago: University of Chicago Press).

Johnson, P. C. (2014) 'International Open Access Week at Small to Medium U.S. Academic Libraries: The First Five Years', *The Journal of Academic Librarianship*, 40(6): 626–31.

'Just Press Print'(25 February 2010) *The Economist*, http://www.economist.com/node/15580856, accessed 10 September 2015.

Kenney, A. R. (2015) 'From Engaging Liaison Librarians to Engaging Communities', *College & Research Libraries*, 76(3): 386–91.

Kirschenbaum, M. (2008) *Mechanisms: New Media and the Forensic Imagination* (Boston: MIT Press).

Knowledge Infrastructures: Intellectual Frameworks and Research Challenges Report and Workshop, http://knowledgeinfrastructures.org/, accessed 15 August 2015.

Lambert, C. (2015) 'The "Wild West" of Academic Publishing: The Troubled Present and Promising Future of Scholarly Communication', *Harvard Magazine*, http://harvardmagazine.com/2015/01/the-wild-west-of-academic-publishing, accessed 25 August 2015.

Lapowsky, I. (2015) 'What Schools Must Learn from LA's iPad Debacle', *Wired*, http://www.wired.com/2015/05/los-angeles-edtech/, accessed 7 August 2015.

Lavik, E. (2012) 'The Video Essay: The Future of Academic Film and Television Criticism?' *Frames #1*, http://framescinemajournal.com/article/the-video-essay-the-future/, accessed 17 August 2015.

Lavoie, B. and C. Malpas (2015) *Stewardship of the Evolving Scholarly Record: From the Invisible Hand to Conscious Coordination* (Dublin, Ohio: OCLC Research), http://www.oclc.org/content/dam/research/publications/2015/oclcresearch-esr-stewardship-2015.pdf, accessed 25 August 2015.

Lederman, D. (2012) 'Fleeing from "Free"', *Inside Higher Ed*, https://www.insidehighered.com/news/2012/11/05/flat-worlds-shift-gears-

and-what-it-means-open-textbook-publishing, accessed 7 August 2015.
Lee, K. B. (2014) 'Video Essay: The Essay Film – Some Thoughts of Discontent', *Sight and Sound*, http://www.bfi.org.uk/news-opinion/sight-sound-magazine/features/deep-focus/video-essay-essay-film-some-thoughts, accessed 15 August 2015.
LIBER (2015) *The Hague Declaration on Knowledge Discovery in the Digital Age*, http://thehaguedeclaration.com, accessed 7 August 2015.
Libres V. (2015) 'Palgrave Pivot: Mopping Up the Mid-Length Manuscripts', *Vulpes Libres* (blog), https://vulpeslibris.wordpress.com/2015/04/29/palgrave-pivot-mopping-up-the-mid-length-manuscripts/, accessed 20 August 2015.
Library Services, King's College London (2015) *Laptop Loans for Students*, http://www.kcl.ac.uk/library/using/loans/laptops.aspx, accessed 22 August 2015.
Mahalek, G. (8 January 2015) 'The University of North Carolina Press Receives Major Grant from Mellon Foundation', *Publisher's Weekly*, http://www.publishersweekly.com/binary-data/NEWS_BRIEFS/attachment/000/000/6-1.pdf, accessed 20 August 2015.
Mak, B. (2011) *How the Page Matters* (Toronto: University of Toronto Press).
Malenfant, K. J. (2010) 'Leading Change in the System of Scholarly Communication: A Case Study of Engaging Liaison Librarians for Outreach to Faculty', *College and Research Libraries*, 71(1): 63–76.
Mathews, B. (2014) 'Librarian as Futurist: Changing the Way Libraries Think About the Future', *Portal: Libraries and the Academy*, 14(3): 453–62.
McCabe, D. (2013) 'Why Bookshops Matter', *The Bookseller*, http://www.thebookseller.com/blogs/why-bookshops-matter, accessed 4 September 2015.
McGann, J. (1991) *The Textual Condition* (Princeton, NJ: Princeton University Press).
Michigan Publishing (April 2015) 'Building a Hosted Platform for Managing Monographic Source Materials and Born Digital Publications through Library/Press Collaboration', *Michigan Publishing website*, http://www.publishing.umich.edu/files/2015/04/Hydra_Fedora_Mellon_Proposal_Summary.pdf, accessed 20 August 2015.
MLA Ad Hoc Committee (2002) *Report on the Future of Scholarly Publishing*, http://www.mla.org/resources/documents/

issues_scholarly_pub/repview_future_pub, accessed 10 September 2015.

Mock, G. (2013) 'Surprising Bright Future for Academic Books" *Duke Today*, https://today.duke.edu/2013/12/dukepress, accessed 25 August 2015.

Moretti, F. (2005) *Graphs, Maps, Trees: Abstract Models for a Literary History* (New York: Verso).

Moretti, F. (2013) *Distant Reading* (New York: Verso).

Nelson, R. (ed.) (2013) *Practice as Research in the Arts: Principles, Protocols, Pedagogies, Resistances* (Basingstoke: Palgrave Macmillan).

Newman, E. (2014) *Simba Information Global Social Science and Humanities Publishing 2013–14 report*, http://www.simbainformation.com/Global-Social-Science-7935107/, accessed 10 September 2015.

Newton, H. (March 2013) 'Breaking Boundaries in Academic Publishing: Launching a New Format for Scholarly Research', *Insights*, 26(1): 70–76.

Newton, H. (28 February 2014) 'Experiment in Open Peer Review for Books Suggests Increased Fairness and Transparency in Feedback Process', *LSE Impact* (blog), http://blogs.lse.ac.uk/impactofsocialsciences/2014/02/28/palgrave-macmillan-open-peer-review-for-book-proposals/, accessed 20 August 2015.

OAPEN-UK (2012) 'Survey of Use of Monographs by Academics – as Authors and Readers', *OAPEN-UK website*, http://oapen-uk.jiscebooks.org/files/2012/02/OAPEN-UK-researcher-survey-final.pdf, accessed 20 August 2015.

OECD (2014) *Education at a Glance 2014: OECD Indicators*, http://www.oecd.org/edu/Education-at-a-Glance-2014.pdf, accessed 9 September 2015.

Oxford English Dictionary (2015) 'Culture, n.' in *OED Online* [database] (Oxford: Oxford University Press), accessed 22 August 2015.

Page, B. (30 July 2015) 'Goldsmiths to Launch "Inventive" University Press', *The Bookseller*, http://www.thebookseller.com/news/goldsmiths-launch-inventive-university-press-308334, accessed 20 August 2015.

Pinfield, S., J. Salter, P. A. Peter and A. Bath (2015) 'The "Total Cost of Publication" in a Hybrid Open-Access Environment: Institutional Approaches to Funding Journal Article-Processing Charges in Combination with Subscriptions', *Journal of the Association for*

Information Science and Technology, http://onlinelibrary.wiley.com/doi/10.1002/asi.23446/epdf, accessed 25 August 2015.

Piper, A. (2012) *Book Was There: Reading in Electronic Times* (Chicago: University of Chicago Press).

Posner, M. (2013) 'No Half Measures: Overcoming Common Challenges to Doing Digital Humanities in the Library', *Journal of Library Administration*, 53: 43–52.

Poynder, R. (8 March 2015) 'The OA Interviews: Alison Mudditt, Director, University of California Press', *Open and Shut?* (blog), http://poynder.blogspot.com/2015/03/the-oa-interviews-alison-mudditt.html, accessed 20 August 2015.

Priem, J., D. Taraborelli, P. Groth and C. Neylon (2010) *Altmetrics: A Manifesto*, http://altmetrics.org/manifesto, accessed 4 September 2015.

Publishers Communications Group (2015) *Library Budget Predictions for 2015*, http://www.pcgplus.com/wp-content/uploads/2015/01/Library-Budget-Predictions-for-2015.pdf, accessed 7 August 2015.

RCUK (2015) 'Unlocking the Future: Open Access Communication in a Global Research Environment', *RCUK website*, http://www.rcuk.ac.uk/media/announcements/150527/, accessed 10 September 2015.

Richter, H. (1992) 'The Film Essay: A New Form of Documentary Film', in Christa Blümlinger and Constatin Wuldd (eds). *Schreiben Bilder Sprechen: Texte zum essayistischen Film* (Vienna: Sonderzahl).

Rowlands, I., D. Nicholas, P. Williams, et al. (2008) 'The Google Generation: The Information Behaviour of the Researcher of the Future', *Aslib Proceedings*, 60(4): 290–310.

Schonfeld, R. C. (2003) *JSTOR: A History* (Princeton, NJ: Princeton University Press).

Seyed Vahid, A. and M. Alireza Isfandyari (2008) 'Bridging the Digital Divide: The Role of Librarians and Information Professionals in the Third Millennium', *The Electronic Library*, 26(2): 226–37.

Showers B. (2014) *A National Monograph Strategy*, http://monographs.jiscinvolve.org/wp/, accessed 10 September 2015.

Silver, I. (2014) 'Authors@UF Campus Conversation Series: A Case Study', *Public Services Quarterly*, 10(4): 263–82.

Sparkes, M. (23 December 2014) 'Internet in North Korea: Everything You Need to Know', *Daily Telegraph*, http://www.telegraph.co.uk/technology/11309882/Internet-in-North-Korea-everything-you-need-to-know.html, accessed 4 September 2015.

Bibliography

Straumsheim, C. (25 February 2015) 'Piecing Together Publishing', *Inside Higher Ed*, https://www.insidehighered.com/news/2015/02/25/researchers-university-press-directors-emboldened-mellon-foundation-interest, accessed 20 August 2015.

Sullivan, G. (2009) *Art Practice as Research: Inquiry in Visual Arts*, 2nd edn (London: Sage).

Tracy, A. et al. (2013) 'The Essay Film', *Sight and Sound*, http://www.bfi.org.uk/news-opinion/sight-sound-magazine/features/deep-focus/essay-film, accessed 15 August 2015.

University of Manchester Library (2015) *My Learning Essentials*, http://www.library.manchester.ac.uk/services-and-support/students/support-for-your-studies/my-learning-essentials, accessed 4 September 2015.

University of Minnesota Press (20 April 2015) 'The University of Minnesota Press partners with CUNY's GC Digital Scholarship Lab to launch MANIFOLD SCHOLARSHIP—a platform for iterative, networked monographs—with grant from the Andrew W. Mellon Foundation', *University of Minnesota Press website*, https://www.upress.umn.edu/press/press-releases/manifold-scholarship, accessed 20 August 2015.

Vandegrift, M. and G. Colvin (2012) 'Relational Communications: Developing Key Connections', *College & Research Libraries News*, 73(7): 386–89.

Vincent N. and C. Wickham (eds) (2013) *Debating Open Access* (London: British Academy).

Vonnegut, K. (1994) *Welcome to the Monkey House, Palm Sunday: An Autobiographical Collage* (London: Vintage Books).

Ware, M. and M. Mabe (2015) *The STM Report – An Overview of Scientific and Scholarly Journal Publishing*, 4th edn (STM, International Association of Scientific, Technical and Medical Publishers).

Webb, K. (17 July 2015) 'The Content that Never Contents', *Times Literary Supplement,*.

Wellmon, C. (2015) *Organizing Enlightenment: Information Overload and the Invention of the Modern Research University* (Baltimore, MD: Johns Hopkins University Press).

Wolf Thomson, J. (2002) 'The Death of the Scholarly Monograph in the Humanities? Citation Patterns in Literary Scholarship', *Libri*, 52: 121–36.

Wolf, M. (2008) *Proust and the Squid: The Story and Science of the Reading Brain* (New York: HarperCollins).

Wright, A. M. (2012) 'Starting Scholarly Conversations: A Scholarly Communication Outreach Program', *Journal of Librarianship and Scholarly Communication*, 2(1): 1–9.

Yang, D. (2013) 'UK Research Reserve: A Sustainable Model from Print to E?', *Library Management*, 34(4/5): 309–23.

Zichuhr, K. (2013) *Who's Not Online and Why* (Washington, DC: Pew Research Center), http://www.pewinternet.org/2013/09/25/whos-not-online-and-why/, accessed 4 September 2014.

Further Reading

Anderson, R. (2014) 'How Important Are University Press Books to the Library? One Case Study', *Scholarly Kitchen* (blog), http://scholarlykitchen.sspnet.org/2014/07/28/how-important-are-university-press-books-to-the-library-one-case-study/, accessed 20 August 2015.

——. (2014) 'University Presses: "Under Fire" or Just Under the Gun (Like the Rest of Us)?', *Scholarly Kitchen* (blog), http://scholarlykitchen.sspnet.org/2014/05/19/university-presses-under-fire-or-just-under-the-gun-like-the-rest-of-us/, accessed 20 August 2015.

——. (2015) 'A Quiet Culture War in Research Libraries – and What It Means for Librarians, Researchers and Publishers', *Insights*, 28(2): 21–7.

August, O. (2007) 'The Great Firewall: China's Misguided – and Futile – Attempt to Control What Happens Online', *Wired*, 15(11), http://archive.wired.com/politics/security/magazine/15-11/ff_chinafirewall, accessed 4 September 2015.

Brown L., R. Griffiths and M. Rascoff (2007) 'University Publishing in a Digital Age', *The Journal of Electronic Publishing*, 10(3).

Carr, N. G. (2010) *The Shallows: How the Internet is Changing the Way We Read, Think and Remember* (London: Atlantic Books).

CILIP (2004) *Ethical Principles*, http://www.cilip.org.uk/cilip/about/ethics/ethical-principles, accessed 22 August 2015.

CLOCKSS (2015) *CLOCKSS Homepage*, https://www.clockss.org, accessed 27 August 2015.

CrossRef (2015), *CrossRef Homepage*, http://www.crossref.org, accessed 27 August 2015.

Darnton, R. (25 April 2013) 'The National Digital Public Library Is Launched.' *The New York Review of Books*, http://www.nybooks.com/articles/archives/2013/apr/25/national-digital-public-library-launched, accessed 4 September 2015

Digital Public Library of America (2015) *DPLA Homepage*, http://dp.la, accessed 24 August 2015.

Directory of Open Access Books (2015) *DOAB Homepage*, http://www.doabooks.org, accessed 24 August 2015.

Durant, D. M. and T. Horova (2014) 'The Future of Reading and Academic Libraries', *Libraries and the Academy*, 15(1): 5–27.

Esposito J. (2007) 'The Wisdom of Oz: The Role of the University Press in Scholarly Communications', *The Journal of Electronic Publishing*, 10(1).

——. (2011) 'Creating a New University', *Scholarly Kitchen* (blog), http://scholarlykitchen.sspnet.org/2011/05/25/creating-a-new-university-press-the-first-of-a-two-part-post/, accessed 20 August 2015.

——. (2013) 'Are University Presses Better Off Now than They Were Four Years Ago?' *Scholarly Kitchen* (blog), http://scholarlykitchen.sspnet.org/2013/06/12/are-university-presses-better-off-now-than-they-were-four-years-ago/, accessed 20 August 2015.

——. (2013) 'Stage Five Book Publishing: A Guide for University Presses', *Scholarly Kitchen* (blog), http://scholarlykitchen.sspnet.org/2013/12/10/stage-five-book-publishing-a-guide-for-university-presses/, accessed 20 August 2015.

European Library (2015) *The European Library Homepage*, http://www.theeuropeanlibrary.org, accessed 24 August 2015.

Eve, M. (2015) *Open Access and the Humanities: Contexts, Controversies and the Future* (Cambridge: Cambridge University Press).

Fisher, R. (2012) 'How Shall We Sing in a Strange Land?' *Logos*, 23(3): 7–15.

Hathi Trust (2015), *Hathi Trust Homepage*, https://www.hathitrust.org, accessed 27 August.

Internet Archive (2015) *The Internet Archive Homepage*, https://archive.org, accessed 27 August.

Library Services, King's College London (2015) *Laptop Loans for Students*, http://www.kcl.ac.uk/library/using/loans/laptops.aspx, accessed 4 September 2015.

Mandler P. (2014) 'Open Access: A Perspective from the Humanities', *Insights*, 27(2): 166–70.

Mrva-Montoya A. (2015) 'Beyond the Monograph: Publishing Research for Multimedia and Multiplatform Delivery', *Journal of Scholarly Publishing*, 46(4): 321–42.

OCLC (2015) *WorldCat Homepage*, https://www.worldcat.org, accessed 27 August 2015.

Portico (2015) *Portico Homepage*, http://www.portico.org, accessed 27 August.

Rowlands, I. D. Nicholas, P. Williams, et al. (2008) 'The Google Generation: The Information Behaviour of the Researcher of the Future', *Aslib Proceedings*, 60(4): 290–310.

Salisbury, L., D. Armato and A. Muddit (9 November 2012) *The Twenty-First Century University Press: Assessing the Past, Envisioning the Future*. Transcription of a live presentation given at the 2012 Charleston Conference on Friday, http://docs.lib.purdue.edu/cgi/viewcontent.cgi?article=1408&context=charleston, accessed 20 August 2015.

Sparkes, M. (23 December 2014) 'Internet in North Korea: Everything You Need to Know', *Daily Telegraph*, http://www.telegraph.co.uk/technology/11309882/Internet-in-North-Korea-everything-you-need-to-know.html, accessed 4 September 2015.

University of Manchester Library (2015) *My Learning Essentials*, http://www.library.manchester.ac.uk/services-and-support/students/support-for-your-studies/my-learning-essentials, accessed 4 September 2015.

Thompson, J. B. (2005) *Books in the Digital Age* (Cambridge: Polity Press).

van der Hoeven, H. and J. van Albada (1996) *Lost Memory – Libraries and Archives Destroyed in the Twentieth Century* (Paris: UNESCO), http://www.unesco.org/webworld/mdm/administ/pdf/LOSTMEMO.PDF, accessed 22 August 2015.

Wikipedia (2015) *List of Book-Burning Incidents*, https://en.wikipedia.org/wiki/List_of_book-burning_incidents, accessed 22 August 2015.

Withey. L, S. Cohn, E. Faran, M. Jensen, G. Kiely, W. Underwood, B. Wilcox, R. Brown, P. Givler, A. Holzman and K. Keane (2011) 'Sustaining Scholarly Publishing: New Business Models for University Presses: A Report of the AAUP Task Force on Economic Models for Scholarly Publishing', *Journal of Scholarly Publishing*, 42(4): 397–441.

Zichuhr, K. (2013) *Who's Not Online and Why* (Washington, DC: Pew Research Center). Also available online: http://www.pewinternet.org/2013/09/25/whos-not-online-and-why/, accessed 4 September 2014.

Index

Academic Book of the Future, 57–63
academic books, 2, 3, 5–7, 15, 20, 21, 57–63, 67–69, 75–77, 80, 89, 98
academy, 6, 13–14, 16, 26, 47, 75
accessibility, 14, 49, 84, 86, 87, 89
AHRC, 2, 3, 8, 63, 71
Amazon, 95
Andrew W. Mellon Foundation, 47, 48, 49, 51, 52, 53, 54
arts and humanities, 12–13, 16, 58–61, 68, 69
assessment, 2, 4, 7, 13, 14, 21, 51, 59, 60, 94
Association of American University Presses (AAUP), 47, 53, 55

Barnes & Noble, 95
Blackwell's, x, 6, 95
Bookboon, 88, 91
book history, 12, 84–90
book supply chain, 39, 41, 44
bookseller, 7, 86, 92–97, 98, 100, 101
bookselling, 3, 84–90
bookshop, 7, 42, 89, 90, 98, 99–103
The British Library, 2, 3, 5, 6, 8, 57, 59, 61–62, 63 n.1, 64, 65, 71, 78

California Digital Library, 49
Cambridge University Press, 33, 34
campus, 7, 70, 94, 98, 100, 101, 102
Canterbury Christ Church University (CCCU), 7, 98, 100–103
CILIP, 79, 80, 81
CLOCSS/LOCKSS, 59, 79
codex, 4, 12–13, 14, 15
collaboration, 12, 58, 61, 62–63, 70, 79, 99
consumer, 6, 22, 85, 89, 90, 93
courseware, 93, 94, 95–97
Crossick, Geoffrey, 8, 51
CrossRef, 79

devices, 15, 16, 44, 76, 80, 89
digital humanities, 18, 22–23
digital preservation, 74, 78, 79
Digital Public Library of America (DPLA), 79, 80
Directory of Open Access Books (DOAB), 79

ebooks, 4, 5, 20, 21, 22, 34, 43–44, 62, 68, 77, 87, 88, 95–96, 99, 100, 101
economics, 76, 78, 85, 86, 96
ethics, 79–80
European Library, 79
evaluation, 4, 7, 95, 96

Flat World, 87
Follett, 95
format, 4, 12, 27, 34, 35, 36–37, 89, 99, 103
funding, 6, 12, 35, 48, 60–61, 86, 87

Global Research Council, 62
Google, 5, 59, 78, 99
Goldsmiths University Press, 37

Harvard University Press, 43
Heath Trust, 79
HEFCE, 28, 35, 70, 73
humanities, 12–13, 15, 16, 18, 21–23, 26, 33, 35, 47, 49, 58–61, 68

innovation, 4, 6, 8, 16, 25, 53, 59, 87–89
The Internet Archive, 79

Jisc, 50, 52, 54, 59
Johns Hopkins University Press, 49
JS Group (also John Smith Group), x, 7
JSTOR, 66, 68

King's College London library, xii, 6, 80, 82
knowledge infrastructures, 5, 39, 40, 41, 42, 44
Knowledge Unlatched, xi, 5, 45, 51, 59
Kortext, 95

learning resources, 92, 93, 94–95, 97
librarianship, 57, 74, 79
libraries, 5–6, 13, 44, 45, 52, 53, 57–63, 67–71, 75, 77–81, 85, 99, 101
library data, 66, 67, 68, 69–70
linked data, 19–20
Liverpool University Press, ix, 5, 51

Manchester University Press, xi, 5, market, 34, 37, 42, 43, 85–90, 96, 97
market research, 32, 34
monograph, 12, 13–14, 16, 20, 22, 23, 33–34, 37, 42–43, 47–51, 61, 62, 67, 70

MOOC, 7, 62, 94, 95
Muse OPEN, 49

national libraries, 5–6, 57–63
New York University Press, 48

OAPEN-UK, 54, 59
Open Access, 2, 5, 6, 8, 12, 27, 37, 47, 48–52, 58–62, 64 n.15, 67, 70, 76, 78, 79, 84, 86–88, 90
OpenIntro, 88
Open Library of the Humanities, 51, 59
Oxford University Press, 87

Palgrave Macmillan, vii, ix, xi, 3, 5, 32–38, 50
Palgrave Pivot, 3, 8, 35–37
peer review, 4, 21, 27, 33, 34, 49, 50, 79, 85, 86
PhD thesis, 14
Policy Press, 37
PORTICO, 59, 79
Practice as Research, 4, 24, 25–28
preservation, 5, 14, 48, 50, 59–60, 62, 78, 79
Princeton University Press, 34
print on demand, 4, 6, 32, 90
printed book, 14, 15, 18, 21, 23, 43, 68
Project Muse, 49
promotion, 13, 14, 19, 75, 100
publisher, 7, 32–35, 37, 40–45, 47, 51–53, 79, 81, 85–90, 94, 101
publishing, 2, 5, 33, 41, 47–52, 67, 68, 85–86, 93

reading, 15–16, 20, 22, 50, 68–69, 77, 84, 94, 100, 103
Research Councils UK (RCUK), 62, 65
Research Excellence Framework (REF), 2, 13, 26, 34, 35, 44, 66, 67, 71 n.7
research output, 4, 14, 28, 35, 59
research policy, 57, 61

Sage, 37
software, 15, 92, 94, 96
Springer, 34
Stanford University Press, 37, 49
student, 16, 51–52, 59, 68, 69, 86–89, 93–97, 98, 99, 100–103
student experience, 7, 51, 98, 99, 101, 102
supply and demand, 6, 41, 85, 86

technology, 3, 14, 22, 28, 33, 52, 78–79, 99
textbook, 7, 51–52, 75, 87–89, 92–96

UCL Press, 45, 52
UK Research Reserve, 66, 68
UKSG, xi
university, 5v, 13–14, 21, 37, 46–53, 67–69, 78, 80, 87, 93, 94, 97, 99–103

University of California Press, 49
University of Chicago Press, 47
University of Manchester Library, 80, 82
University of Michigan Press, 49, 54
University of Minnesota Press, 49, 53
University of North Carolina Press, 48, 53
University of Nottingham library, xii, 6, 66, 67, 69

Vega, 50
video essay, 4, 24, 26, 27–28

Wikipedia, 21, 78, 93
WorldCat, 79

Yale University Press, 49
Yuzu, 95

The manufacturer's authorised representative in the EU is Springer Nature Customer Service Centre GmbH, Europaplatz 3, 69115 Heidelberg, Germany. If you have any concerns regarding our products, please contact ProductSafety@springernature.com

Printed and bound by CPI Group (UK) Ltd, Croydon, CR0 4YY

23/03/2026

02076355-0013